MAY 2016

I0084537

India in a Reconnecting Eurasia

Foreign Economic and Security Interests

AUTHOR
Gulshan Sachdeva

EDITOR
Jeffrey Mankoff

Eurasia from the Outside In

A REPORT OF THE
CSIS RUSSIA AND EURASIA PROGRAM

CSIS | CENTER FOR STRATEGIC & INTERNATIONAL STUDIES

ROWMAN & LITTLEFIELD
Lanham • Boulder • New York • London

About CSIS

For over 50 years, the Center for Strategic and International Studies (CSIS) has worked to develop solutions to the world's greatest policy challenges. Today, CSIS scholars are providing strategic insights and bipartisan policy solutions to help decisionmakers chart a course toward a better world.

CSIS is a nonprofit organization headquartered in Washington, D.C. The Center's 220 full-time staff and large network of affiliated scholars conduct research and analysis and develop policy initiatives that look into the future and anticipate change.

Founded at the height of the Cold War by David M. Abshire and Admiral Arleigh Burke, CSIS was dedicated to finding ways to sustain American prominence and prosperity as a force for good in the world. Since 1962, CSIS has become one of the world's preeminent international institutions focused on defense and security; regional stability; and transnational challenges ranging from energy and climate to global health and economic integration.

Thomas J. Pritzker was named chairman of the CSIS Board of Trustees in November 2015. Former U.S. deputy secretary of defense John J. Hamre has served as the Center's president and chief executive officer since 2000.

CSIS does not take specific policy positions; accordingly, all views expressed herein should be understood to be solely those of the author(s).

ISBN: 978-1-4422-5938-6 (pb); 978-1-4422-5939-3 (eBook)

Center for Strategic & International Studies
1616 Rhode Island Avenue, NW
Washington, DC 20036
202-887-0200 | www.csis.org

Rowman & Littlefield
4501 Forbes Boulevard
Lanham, MD 20706
301-459-3366 | www.rowman.com

Contents

Preface

In January 2014, the CSIS Russia and Eurasia Program launched its Eurasia Initiative. The vast Eurasian landmass, stretching from China in the east to Europe in the west and from the Arctic Ocean in the north to the Indian Ocean in the south, includes some of the world's most powerful and dynamic states, as well as some of the world's most intractable challenges. Scholars and analysts are accustomed to focusing separately on Eurasia's various regions—Europe, the former Soviet Union, East Asia, South Asia, and Southeast Asia—rather than on the interactions between them. The goal of this initiative is to focus on these interactions, while analyzing and understanding Eurasia in a comprehensive way.

Today, more than any time since the collapse of the Silk Road five centuries ago, understanding these individual regions is impossible without also understanding the connections between them. Over the past two decades, Eurasia has begun to slowly reconnect, with the emergence of new trade relationships and transit infrastructures, as well as the integration of Russia, China, and India into the global economy. Even as this reconnection is under way, the center of economic dynamism in Eurasia, and in the world as a whole, continues shifting to the East. The impact of these shifts is potentially enormous, but they remain poorly understood because of intellectual and bureaucratic stovepiping in government and the broader analytic community.

Following its twin report series on Central Asia and on the South Caucasus, respectively, the CSIS Russia and Eurasia Program is now releasing papers in a third series we are informally calling "Eurasia from the Outside In." If the first two Eurasia Initiative report series focused on how economic connectivity and shifting political alignments looked from the interior of Eurasia, the current series focuses on the perspectives of the large, powerful countries that make up the periphery of the Eurasian landmass, namely China, India, Iran, Russia, and Turkey, as well as the European Union. The six reports in this series, each written by a leading local scholar of Eurasia, seek to provide insight into where Eurasia fits among the foreign economic and security priorities of these major powers.

While the most visible components of Eurasia's reconnection are infrastructure projects, the longer term result has been a reshuffling of relations between the post-Soviet states of Central

Asia and the South Caucasus on the one hand, and the major regional powers on the other. When the states of Central Asia and the South Caucasus became independent 25 years ago, they were closely tied to Russia. Over the past two and a half decades, they have developed a complex web of linkages to the other Eurasian powers, who themselves have devoted increased resources and attention to Eurasia in the years since the Soviet collapse. Russia still remains the dominant security provider in Central Asia and most of the South Caucasus. However China, the European Union, India, Iran, and Turkey all play major, if still evolving, roles in the region as well.

The scholars we have commissioned to write these reports bring a deep knowledge of their respective countries as well as a strong understanding of developments across Eurasia. While they are addressing a common set of questions, their answers and perspectives often diverge. Our goal is not consensus. Rather, it is to provide the best possible analysis of the roles these states are playing in shaping Eurasia's reconnection. We chose to seek out scholars from the countries being studied so that these reports would not be U.S.-centric, but would rather throw light on how Ankara, Beijing, Brussels, Moscow, New Delhi, and Tehran conceive of their respective interests and strategies in Eurasia.

With this report series, and indeed with the Eurasia Initiative more generally, we hope to encourage analysts and policymakers to think about Eurasia in a holistic way. Eurasia is much more than just the periphery of the old Soviet Union: it is a patchwork of states and peoples whose relationships are shifting rapidly. It is Central Asia, but it is also Europe; the South Caucasus but also India. Most importantly, it is the connections that are emerging and developing between these various states and regions. Our "Eurasia from the Inside Out" report series highlights the extent to which the comparatively small states at Eurasia's center have become a focal point for the economic and political engagement of the much larger powers surrounding them, and hence why these states continue to matter for global peace and prosperity.

Acknowledgments

This report is made possible by the generous support of the Smith Richardson Foundation, the Carnegie Corporation of New York, the Ministry of Foreign Affairs of the Republic of Kazakhstan, and Carlos Bulgheroni. We are also extremely grateful for program support provided by the Carnegie Corporation of New York to the CSIS Russia and Eurasia Program.

The View from New Delhi

Most Indian policymakers and analysts believe that the South Caucasus and Central Asia are important because of their strategic location, cultural and civilizational linkages with India, energy resources, and the trade and other economic opportunities they offer.[1] The geopolitical salience of Eurasia for India was never in doubt. Developing political, economic, and energy partnerships dominated India's "extended neighborhood"[2] policy in the post-Soviet period. The Chinese and Afghanistan factors have increased the region's strategic significance for New Delhi considerably in the last 15 years.

These realities pushed Indian policymakers to expand and vigorously implement India's "Connect Central Asia" policy announced in 2012. Focusing on Eurasia's location, oil and gas reserves, and competition for pipeline routes, many Indian analysts advanced the narrative of a New Great Game (i.e., strategic competition between the major powers for access to and influence in Central Eurasia) in the 1990s. Later, the competition for military bases in Central Asia, as well as fears of revolution and regime change, added a new dimension to this struggle for influence among the various powers.

Despite its rhetoric and sometimes intentions, India itself was never really part of any competition for influence in the region. Some scholars accused India of indulging in wishful thinking toward the region, rather than developing a coherent strategy.[3] With no direct road transportation access plus difficult market conditions, the South Caucasus and Central Asia did not become attractive to Indian private companies. In the 1990s, economic relationships with the region also declined considerably.

---

1. Tajikistan is just about 20 kilometers from Greater Kashmir.

2. India's growing capacity and will to project hard and soft power in subregions beyond South Asia. See David Scott, "India's 'Extended Neighborhood' Concept: Power Projection for Rising Power," *India Review* 8, no. 2 (2009): 107–143.

3. Emilian Kavalski, *India and Central Asia: The Mythmaking and International Relations of a Rising Power* (London: I. B. Tauris, 2010).

Politically, Indian officials were more or less comfortable dealing with authoritarian leaders in the region. These leaders were part of the former Soviet elite, with whom India had dealt for decades. They moreover appeared to provide stability and were committed to fight Islamist extremism and terrorism. Unlike the United States, Europe, and many multilateral organizations seeking to spread democracy and market economics in the region, India has been focused primarily on ensuring political stability, because an unstable Eurasia is a serious threat for New Delhi. India obviously would have welcomed a more democratic Central Asia, but it favored allowing democratization to happen at its own pace. New Delhi also remained convinced that Russia would retain a predominant political and economic influence in the region, and generally pursued cooperation with Moscow in Central Asia and the Caucasus.

Although many in India still believe in the continuation of Russia's overwhelming influence in the region, many scholars have also started considering another possibility in which, over time, China would become a dominant player in the region while becoming increasingly friendly to Russia. As China increases its engagement in the region and creates a larger profile through trade, energy deals, military agreements, the Shanghai Cooperation Organization (SCO), and now the One Belt One Road (OBOR) project, India is watching carefully.[4] Despite many positive developments and fruitful diplomatic engagements, India is still very cautious in matters relating China. Both New Delhi and Beijing are still very much concerned with basic balance-of-power considerations, although officially both deny this proposition.

Persistent uncertainty in Afghanistan, particularly in the context of difficult India-Pakistan relations, has also added a new dimension to India's approach to Eurasia. Though the failure of the international project to stabilize Afghanistan poses common security challenges, any positive outcome will open tremendous economic opportunities to both India and Central Asia. Though the Caucasus is much more peripheral for Indian interests, Azerbaijan's attempts to emerge as a trade and transportation hub[5] in particular afford New Delhi an opportunity to take advantage of the South Caucasus region to reorient some of its trade and transit routes.

Today New Delhi's approach to the region is laid out in the Connect Central Asia initiative, first announced in 2012. This initiative seeks to strengthen India's political, security, economic, and cultural connections with Central Asia. As outlined by the minister of state for external affairs, E Ahmed, at the first India Central Asia Dialogue in Bishkek on June 12, 2012, the policy comprises 12 points:[6]

- Further strengthening political relations with the region
- Strengthening strategic and security cooperation (through military training, joint research, counterterrorism cooperation, and close consultations on Afghanistan)

---

4. Gulshan Sachdeva, "India's Attitude towards China's Growing Influence in Central Asia," *China and Eurasia Forum Quarterly* 4, no. 3 (2006): 23–34, http://www.jnu.ac.in/SIS/MakingSISVisible/Presentations/China%20in%20Central%20 Asia.pdf.

5. Taleh Ziadov, *Azerbaijan as a Regional Hub in Eurasia: Strategic Assessment of Euro-Asian Trade and Transportation* (Baku: Azerbaijan Diplomatic Academy, 2012).

6. For details, see Shri E. Ahamed, "India's 'Connect Central Asia' Policy" (keynote address at First India–Central Asia Dialogue, Bishkek, Kyrgyzstan, June 12, 2012), http://goo.gl/Ku3lIA.

- Stepping up multilateral engagement via the SCO and Eurasian Economic Union (EAEU)

- Developing partnerships in energy and natural resources

- Strengthening cooperation in the medical field

- Establishing a new Central Asian University in Bishkek

- Setting up a Central Asian e-network with its hub in India

- Strengthening private partnerships in sectors like construction and iron and steel

- Reactivating the International North-South Trade Corridor (INSTC)

- Strengthening cooperation in the banking sector

- Improving air connectivity

- Encouraging regular academic exchanges and civil society contacts

The aims of this policy were (1) dealing with the region collectively in a much more proactive manner; (2) strengthening security and defense dialogues with the region, particularly in the context of the U.S. drawdown from Afghanistan and declining interest in Central Asia; (3) exploring possibilities for cooperative engagements with Russia, China, and Iran (both bilaterally and collectively) to safeguard and promote Indian interests; and (4) enlarging India's development cooperation footprint in the region.

The perception of Central Asia's growing strategic significance for India is reflected in Prime Minister Narendra Modi's eight-day visit to all five Central Asian states in July 2015. This was the first visit of any Indian prime minister to all the Central Asian countries simultaneously since they became independent in 1991. The visit also provided a new strategic direction to the Connect Central Asia policy. Earlier, in June 2015, India and the EAEU, consisting of Armenia, Belarus, Kazakhstan, Kyrgyzstan, and Russia, agreed to set up a Joint Study Group.[7] The group will submit its report within a year regarding feasibility of a free trade agreement between India and the EAEU.

New Delhi's growing attention to the region is in no small part a response to the changing dynamics of the major powers' relations with Central Asia. Increased Chinese investment and diplomatic engagement, Russia's economic downturn and the resulting decline in remittances to Central Asia, and the reduced U.S. military focus on Afghanistan have all pushed India to pay more attention to the region.

Particularly important in this context is the increased involvement of China, a country India still regards as a strategic competitor. In 2013, Chinese president Xi Jinping made a 10-day visit to four Central Asian countries and signed an estimated $48 billion worth of investment and loan agreements in the areas of energy, trade, and infrastructure. This investment is designed to create a platform for China's ambitious OBOR initiative linking Asia and Africa with Europe through a network of six transportation corridors, a project that could fundamentally reshape the

---

7. "India, EEU Sets Up Group to Look at Feasibility of FTA," *Economic Times*, June 22, 2015, http://goo.gl/VZnMmJ.

geoeconomics and geopolitics of the whole Eurasian region. Both China and Russia have also made political statements of integrating the EAEU and the OBOR.[8]

In these circumstances, many countries in Eurasia are also looking for enhanced strategic and economic engagement from India. Deepening ties with New Delhi also fits well with the "multi-vector" foreign policies of most Central Asian states, which are trying to balance their dependence on Russia and China through enhanced engagement with other powers. Moreover, India is seen as a benign power that does not pose any ideological, demographic, or territorial threat to the countries in the region.[9] In the last 15 years, Central Asia's trade and investment links with neighboring economic centers have increased significantly. China, Russia, and the European Union (EU) have been main export destinations and sources of imports, foreign direct investment (FDI), and remittances.[10] Now when these economies are either stagnant or slowing down, India could emerge as an attractive market for the Caucasus and Central Asia.

8. "Russia, China Agree to Integrate Eurasian Union, Silk Road, Sign Deals," RT, May 8, 2015, https://www.rt.com/business/256877-russia-china-deals-cooperation/.

9. Rajiv Sikri, *Challenge and Strategy: Rethinking India's Foreign Policy* (New Delhi: Sage, 2009), 165.

10. Asian Development Bank (ADB) Institute, *Connecting Central Asia with Economic Centers* (Tokyo: ADB Institute, 2014), http://www.adb.org/sites/default/files/publication/159307/adbi-connecting-central-asia-economic-centers-final-report.pdf.

India's Foreign Economic and Security Policy

India's economic and security engagements with the outside world have undergone a serious transformation in the last 25 years. India's emergence as a significant international player is mainly due to changes in the global and Asian balance of power, as well as the intensification of global integration, technical changes, and increasing trends toward regional economic integration. India itself is meanwhile making a successful transition from an inward-oriented economy to a more globally integrated economy. As a result India has become one of the fastest-growing economies of the world in the past two and a half decades.[1]

Despite some serious challenges like a global economic slowdown, energy security, poverty, infrastructure, regional disparities, and internal security, there are strong indications that rapid growth will continue. Although growth in the last 10 to 15 years has raised expectations, global circumstances are less favorable today. As a result, India is adapting itself simultaneously to economic globalization and to the shifting balance of power both globally and in Eurasia.

The strategic consequences of India's improved economic performance are clearly evident. Growth and outward orientation have helped India to reorient its traditional partnerships with the developing world as well as forge new relationships with many major powers. Apart from a "special and privileged" partnership with Russia, India has already signed strategic partnerships with Kazakhstan (2009), Uzbekistan (2011), Afghanistan (2011), and Tajikistan (2012). In addition, it has

---

1. The last 25 years' growth has broken all recent trends. Between 1900 and 1950, the Indian economy grew on average 0.8 percent a year. As the population also grew at the same pace, per capita income was almost stagnant. See Gurcharan Das, "India: How a Rich Nation Became Poor and Will Be Rich Again," in *Developing Cultures: Case Studies*, ed. Lawrence E. Harrison and Peter L. Berger (London: Routledge, 2006), 141–162. Between 1950 and 1980 the average economic growth was about 3.6 percent per year. With limited liberalization, economic growth accelerated to about 5.6 percent per year in the 1980s. Since 1990, however, the average economic growth is above 6.5 percent per year in the last 25 years. Just before the global economic slowdown in 2008–2009, the Indian economy was growing at about 9 percent per year for five years. Figures are author's calculations based on data released by the Indian Ministry of Finance. See Indian Ministry of Finance, *Economic Survey 2014–15*, Table 1.2 (New Delhi: Ministry of Finance, 2015), A3–A4, http://indiabudget.nic.in/vol1_survey.asp.

elevated its relations with Mongolia to a "comprehensive partnership" (2015). Interestingly, India and China also established a "strategic and cooperative partnership for peace and prosperity" in 2005. In addition to these bilateral arrangements, India has been playing an important role in the Brazil–Russia–India–China–South Africa (BRICS), India–Brazil–South Africa (IBSA), Russia-India-China (RIC) and Group of 20 (G20) forums. Within Eurasia, India has also been participating in the Conference on Interaction and Confidence-Building Measures in Asia (CICA) and the SCO (which it is expected to join as a full member in 2016) and has engaged in Afghanistan-centric forums like the Regional Economic Cooperation Conferences on Afghanistan (RECCA) and the Heart of Asia process.

Against this backdrop of an emerging India, Prime Minister Narendra Modi received a massive mandate in the 2014 parliamentary elections, mainly on the promise of good governance and development. Hence, his agenda has been to accelerate economic growth through better performance. The Bharatiya Janata Party's (BJP) election manifesto criticized 10 years of "jobless growth" by the previous government and promised to focus on manufacturing, agriculture, infrastructure, and housing. Given these concerns, Modi's government was widely expected to concentrate more on the domestic front.

Unexpectedly, however, Modi has pursued a very active foreign policy as well. As of January 2016, Modi has visited 37 countries in five continents. As former foreign secretary Kanwal Sibal wrote recently, "Modi has energetically expanded the political, security and economic reach of Indian diplomacy."[2] During all his visits abroad, Modi has emphasized the importance of commerce as part of his foreign policy. The focus of his major visits to the United States, Russia, Japan, China, France, Germany, the United Kingdom, South Korea, Singapore, and the United Arab Emirates has been to attract foreign direct investment, pave the way for Indian companies to make investments, and purchase military hardware. India had forged partnerships with several major powers in the last two decades, and Modi has further energized many of them. As leading Indian strategist Brahma Chellaney argued, Modi is "shaping a nondoctrinaire foreign-policy approach powered by ideas," has taken "some of his domestic ideas (such as 'Make in India' and 'Digital India') to foreign policy," and overall is "taking India from non-alignment to multi-alignment."[3]

Many analysts now believe that the Asian continent is on its way to becoming the new center of gravity in global politics. In an evolving Asian economic and security architecture, many Asian countries would be looking toward China or India as the anchor for their future economic and security alignments.[4] As an economic and military superpower, the United States would also like to play an important role in this evolving situation. In the Eurasian region, India will likely play the role of a counterbalance against the backdrop of increasing Chinese dominance and a relatively declining Russian presence. As Enders Wimbush predicted, "India may not be in the same league as

---

2. Kanwal Sibal, "The Modi Style of Diplomacy: Many Hits and Some Misses," *Hindustan Times*, December 31, 2015, http://goo.gl/yXYi1J.

3. Brahma Chellaney, "The Global Pragmatist," *Open Magazine*, May 22, 2015, http://www.openthemagazine.com/article/voices/narendra-modi-the-global-pragmatist.

4. See Ashley J. Tellis, Travis Tanner, and Jessica Keough, eds., *Strategic Asia 2011–12: Asia Responds to Its Rising Powers: China and India* (Washington, DC: National Bureau of Asian Research, 2011).

China or Russia, nor half so visible, but is potentially a future balancer of either or both."[5] So in a rapidly evolving situation, "India would need to bring to bear its rapidly increasing political, economic and military capabilities to the table as a threshold great power with vital stakes in the region."[6]

RUSSIA

Overall, the main pillars of the Indo-Russian relationship are strategic congruence, defense ties, nuclear power, and hydrocarbons. Except for a very brief period of the early 1990s, India and Russia have maintained excellent political relations. In 2000, the two countries signed a strategic partnership agreement, upgraded to a "special and privileged strategic partnership" in 2010.[7] Prime Minister Modi recently went so far as to note that "even a child in India, if asked to say who is India's best friend, will reply it is Russia because Russia has been with India in times of crisis."[8] In the 16 summits held since 2000, New Delhi and Moscow have signed more than 150 agreements and memoranda of understandings and declaration, including in the areas of military and technical cooperation, space, nuclear energy, hydrocarbons, trade and economics, terrorism, education, and culture. Russia is India's major supplier of arms, and partner in nuclear energy.[9]

On the Ukrainian crisis, India has pursued a "balanced" position of emphasizing its respect for the sovereignty and territorial integrity of other countries but also supports Russia's "legitimate interest" in the region.[10] As India never supported unilateral sanctions against any country, it did not support Western sanctions against Russia. Along with China and South Africa, it also abstained at the UN General Assembly from the resolution on Ukraine. In comparison, commercial ties remain underdeveloped. Despite many ambitious targets set by various summits, annual bilateral trade remains below $10 billion and Russian companies have invested only about $1 billion in India so far.

Across the Caucasus and Central Asia, Russia has been and will continue to be an important factor for India. Attempts by Russia to integrate the region under its influence are for the most part viewed positively by New Delhi. India worries that space vacated by a Russian geopolitical retreat would likely be filled by its strategic rival China—or worse, by radical forces. Moreover, for India it is easier to work with Russia in Central Asia than with any other regional or extraregional power. In

---

5. S. Enders Wimbush, "Great Games in Central Asia," in *Strategic Asia 2011–12*, ed. Tellis, Tanner, and Keough, 259–282.

6. Kapil Kak, "India's Strategic and Security Interests in Central Asia," in *Central Asia: Present Challenges & Future Prospects*, ed. V. Nagendra Rao and Mohammad Monir Alam (New Delhi: Knowledge World, 2005), 205–222.

7. For background of Indo-Soviet and then India-Russia relations, see Gulshan Sachdeva, "India's Relations with Russia," in *Handbook of India's International Relations*, ed. David Scott (London: Routledge, 2011), 213–222.

8. "Top 8 Things PM Narendra Modi said at BRICS Summit," *Times of India*, July 16, 2014, http://goo.gl/PFPd2b.

9. According to the Stockholm International Peace Research Institute (SIPRI) arms transfer database, at 1990 constant prices, India imported about $34 billion of weapons from Russia between 1992 and 2014. This was 65 percent of total arms imports by India during this period. Since 2007, India is the largest export market of Russian weapons. See http://www.sipri.org/databases/armstransfers.

10. "Russian Interests in Crimea Legitimate: India," *Times of India*, March 7, 2014, http://goo.gl/S91W2U.

bilateral summit declarations, India and Russia have agreed regularly on the need for strengthening bilateral and multilateral interactions in Central Asia.[11] In the long run, India will be much more supportive of Russian integration designs in Central Asia and the Caucasus than even China, as Indian and Russian interests do not clash with each other in the region.

CHINA

Like their counterparts in most other Asian countries, the biggest challenge for Indian policymakers involves managing relations with China. At the moment, there is a huge asymmetry between the two economies. As a result, the "Chinese are relaxed about the rise of India" but "the Indians are much more nervous about the rise of China."[12] Because both are rising powers in the same part of the world, there are bound to be tensions. Many scholars have posited that India-China relations consist of three Cs: conflict, competition, and cooperation. One of the main sources of tension between India and China is their disputed border. In 1993, an agreement on the maintenance of peace and tranquility along the Line of Actual Control (LAC) was signed, and so far 18 rounds of talks on the boundary question have been held. Incidents of Chinese troops crossing over to Indian territory are common, but the governments have played down these incidents. China has also forged strong relations with many of India's South Asian neighbors, including an "all weather" friendship with Pakistan. Due to its centralized state control system and deep pockets, China is far more successful than India in its natural resource diplomacy. Bilateral economic relations have become stronger. Currently, China is India's number one trading partner, with more than $70 billion trade. However, this trade is hugely tilted in favor of China. It is also likely that China will participate in India's expanding infrastructure.

Expanding economic ties, however, may not necessarily reduce tensions. New Delhi believes that China has transferred nuclear and missile technology to Pakistan, so that India is bottled up in South Asia. With Pakistan further blocking India westward, Indian access to Afghanistan and Central Asia becomes difficult. This provides China a relatively free space in Eurasia, as its rivalry with Beijing's ally Pakistan limits India's influence in and access to the region.

China's signature initiative in the region is the OBOR, which aims to connect more than 60 countries of Asia and Africa with Europe through multiple economic corridors with projected outward

---

11. See "Delhi Declaration on Further Consolidation of Strategic Partnership between the Republic of India and the Russian Federation," December 4, 2002, http://goo.gl/qSxUPw. The declaration clearly stated that "both sides have a vital interest in maintaining security, stability and a secular order in the Central Asian region." A 2007 Russia-India joint statement asserted that both are "interested in strengthening bilateral and multilateral interaction in Central Asia, which would contribute to enhanced stability and security in the region, including through closer and mutually beneficial cooperation with individual countries in the region." See "Joint Statement on the outcome of the Official Visit of H.E. Mr. Vladimir V. Putin, President of the Russian Federation to the Republic of India," Republic of India Ministry of External Affairs, January 25, 2007, http://goo.gl/hclUuH.

12. Charles Grant, "India's Response to China's Rise" (policy brief, Centre for European Reform, August 2010), http://www.cer.org.uk/sites/default/files/publications/attachments/pdf/2011/pb_india_china_grant_aug10-206.pdf.

investments of $500 billion.[13] Out of the proposed six international corridors constituting OBOR,[14] four corridors, namely, the new Eurasia Land Bridge; the China–Central Asia–West Asia Economic Corridor; the China-Pakistan Economic Corridor; and the Bangladesh-China-India-Myanmar Economic Cooperation, directly affect India-Eurasia economic and strategic linkages. One source of concern in New Delhi is that the China-Pakistan Economic Corridor crosses disputed territory in Pakistani-controlled Kashmir.

At the moment there is less clarity in Indian policy circles on how to respond to the OBOR initiative as a whole. As suggested by former foreign secretary Shyam Saran,[15] India may support some of the initiatives, as they will help regional integration and infrastructure building. In the medium run, it seems that India will have to come out with its own similar initiative covering West Asia, the Indian Ocean, and Eurasia. New Delhi is also aware that "no single power—not even the United States—can offset China's power and influence on its own."[16] Meanwhile India will be building close partnerships with those countries that worry about China's ascendancy. And nations that are worried about assertive China have multiplied in the last few years.

IRAN

India shares strong historical and civilizational ties with Iran. Next to Iran, India has the second-largest population of Shi'a Muslims globally (around one-quarter of India's 172 million Muslims, or more than 40 million).[17] Iran also has been one of India's major sources of energy. In the last 15 years, however, relations with Iran have become increasingly vexed by the simultaneous growth of Indo-American ties and Washington's own Iran obsession. Nor have Indians' desire to have cordial relations with other players in the Middle East, many of whom have their own troubles with Iran, made things easy for New Delhi. During the Afghan conflict, India and Iran worked together to back the Northern Alliance in Afghanistan, although they have had diverging opinions about the presence of the North Atlantic Treaty Organization (NATO) and American forces.

Despite Western sanctions, India sought to maintain commercial and energy ties. Still, oil imports from Iran slipped from 16.4 percent of total Indian oil imports in 2008–2009[18] to 5.2 percent in

13. He Yafei, "Connecting the World through Belt and Road," *China-US Focus*, October 13, 2015, http://www.chinausfocus.com/foreign-policy/the-belt-road-initiative-offers-new-model-of-cooperation-in-global-governance/.

14. "The Belt and Road Initiative," HKTDC Research, January 21, 2016, http://china-trade-research.hktdc.com/business-news/article/One-Belt-One-Road/The-Belt-and-Road-Initiative/obor/en/1/1X000000/1X0A36B7.htm.

15. Shyam Saran, "What China's One Belt and One Road Strategy Means for India, Asia and the World," *The Wire*, October 9, 2015, http://goo.gl/fMio5N.

16. Brahma Chellaney, "Upholding the Asian Order," Project Syndicate, January 22, 2016, http://www.project-syndicate.org/commentary/asian-powers-cooperation-for-regional-order-by-brahma-chellaney-2016-01.

17. "World Shia Muslims Population," ShiaNumbers.com, n.d., http://shianumbers.com/index.html.

18. Nidhi Verma, "India's Country-wise Crude Oil Imports Since 2001/02," Reuters, August 6, 2012, http://in.reuters.com/article/india-crude-import-idINL4E8IU4HI20120806.

Map 2.1. India–Iran–Afghanistan–Central Asia Corridor

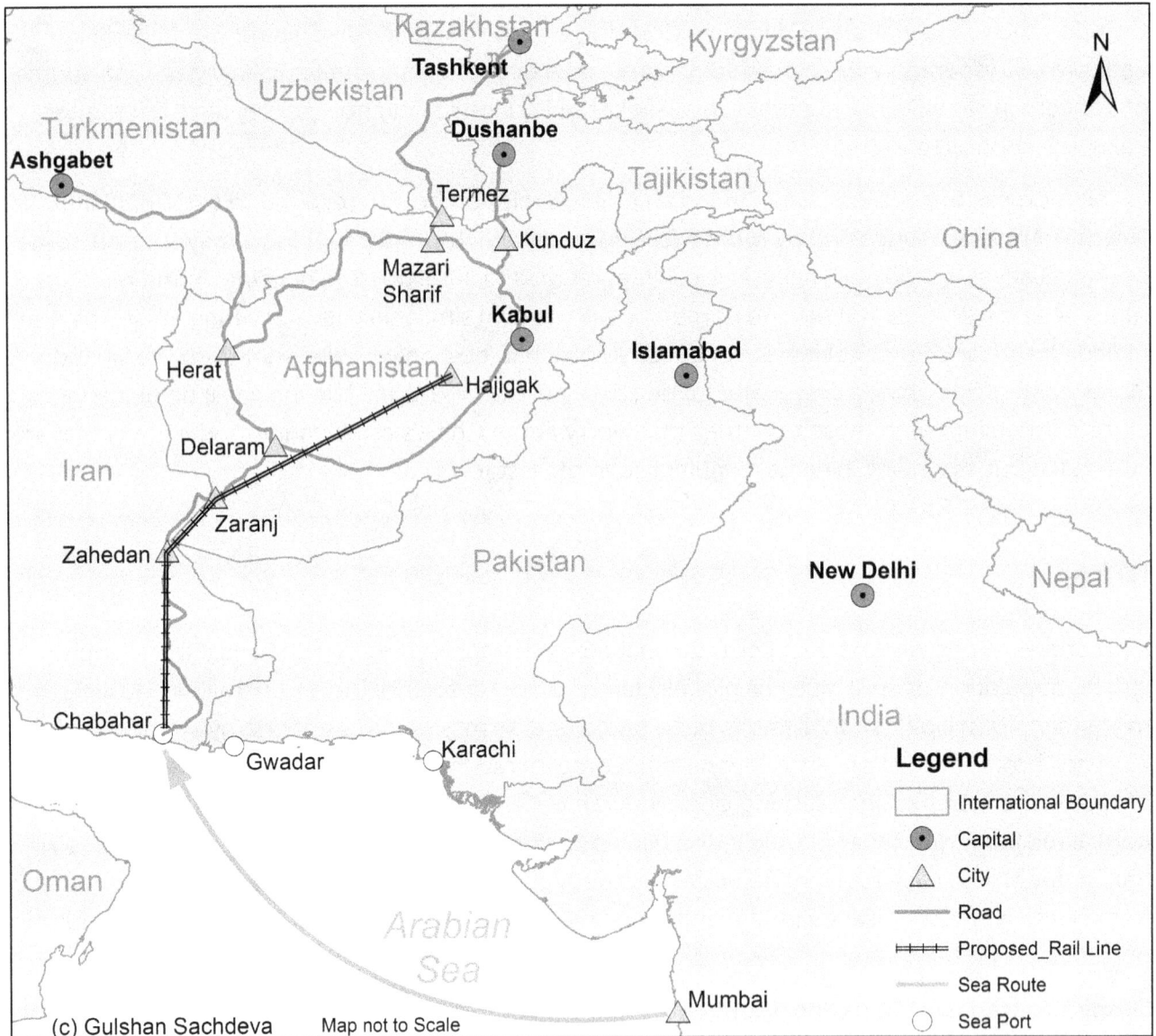

(c) Gulshan Sachdeva   Map not to Scale

Legend

- ☐ International Boundary
- ⊙ Capital
- △ City
- — Road
- ┼┼┼┼ Proposed_Rail Line
- — Sea Route
- ○ Sea Port

2015.[19] The nuclear agreement between Iran and the international community and removal of sanctions will definitely boost bilateral ties.

With the removal of sanctions, Indian oil majors will be more likely to purchase Iranian oil and make investments in Iranian oil fields where they have already made discoveries. This will also help India to expand its options in Eurasia. Due to difficult India-Pakistan relations, Iran has been and will continue to be a crucial part of Indian strategy toward Central Asia and the Caucasus.[20] The establishment of the INSTC and participation in the construction of the Chabahar port in Iran (discussed in more detail in the next chapter) have been part of an Indian strategy to connect

---

19. Nidhi Verma, "India's Dec Oil Imports up 7 Pct y/y—Trade Data," Reuters, January 15, 2016, http://in.reuters.com /article/india-oil-imports-idINL3N14Y59G.

20. See Meena Singh Roy, "Iran: India's Gateway to Central Asia," *Strategic Analysis* 36, no. 6 (November 2012): 957–975.

Central Asia while bypassing Pakistan. The 215-kilometer (km) Zeranj-Delaram highway built by India in Afghanistan also connects the Afghan ring road to the Chabahar port, allowing India to connect it further with Central Asia in the future (see Map 2.1).

EUROPEAN UNION

With the advent of the Cold War, nonalignment, and New Delhi's closeness to the then Soviet Union, India's interactions with Europe became limited. After the Cold War, India's vision of a democratic, multicultural and multipolar world coincided in important ways with that of the European Union. Realizing the importance, Brussels and New Delhi signed a strategic partnership in 2004 followed by a Joint Action Plan in 2005. Since 2007, they have also been negotiating a Broad Based Trade and Investment Agreement. Despite initial enthusiasm, the relationship has lost momentum in recent years. Many factors, including deadlock in trade negotiations, the global slowdown, and the euro zone crisis, have contributed.

The core of the India-EU relationship remains economics. With more than $130 billion of trade in goods and services, the European Union is India's biggest trading partner. In the last 15 years, FDI from the EU member states to India has been higher than investments from the United States and Japan combined. Moreover, Europe has emerged as an important destination for cross-border investments and overseas acquisitions for Indian companies.[21] Most Indian policymakers and analysts are, however, skeptical of the European Union's role as a strategic player in Asia. The European Union is hardly a factor in India's foreign policy debates. Many in India believe that the European Union provides relatively little added value to India's major security challenges related to China, South and Central Asia, and the Middle East. Still, for many years India regarded the European Union as a role model in regional cooperation and a significant player in norm setting. The euro crisis and the European Union's lack of strategic vision as reflected during the Ukrainian crisis, however, have significantly affected the European Union's image in India.

On strategic matters, India has yet to discover the relevance of the India-EU partnership in an evolving Asian security and economic architecture. Rapidly growing Indo-American relations coupled with the close transatlantic partnership could, however, provide new opportunities for Brussels and New Delhi to work together. On defense and security matters, India deals directly with member states, especially with the major European powers France, Germany, and the United Kingdom. India's recent decision to buy Rafale jets from France will have serious long-term positive implications for its ties with Europe.

The European Union adopted a "Strategy for a New Enhanced Partnership with Central Asia" in 2007 and launched its Eastern Partnership, which includes the South Caucasus, in 2009. However, no serious consultations on Eurasia have taken place between India and the European Union, although Brussels supports efforts to integrate Central Asia with South Asia as part of its wider policy of encouraging regional cooperation.

---

21. Gulshan Sachdeva, *Evaluation of the EU-India Strategic Partnership and the Potential for Its Revitalization* (Brussels: Foreign Affairs Committee, European Parliament, 2015).

THE UNITED STATES

A major transformation has taken place in India's relations with the United States during the last 10 years. For most of the Cold War period, India and the United States were "estranged democracies," and engagement between the two only accelerated during the 1980s, as successive U.S. presidents recognized India's potential to shape the emerging balance of power in Asia.[22] U.S. president George W. Bush and Indian prime minister Manmohan Singh laid a foundation for a productive strategic partnership through civil nuclear and defense framework agreements in the mid-2000s. Prime Minister Modi has further energized the relationship.[23] Currently, more than 40 bilateral dialogue mechanisms are in place. Defense cooperation is emerging as an important pillar of the relationship, encompassing arms purchases, joint exercises, collaboration in maritime security, and exchanges between all branches of the two countries' armed services. According to the Indian foreign office, bilateral ties "have developed into a 'global strategic partnership,' based on shared democratic values and increasing convergence of interests on bilateral, regional and global issues."[24]

To a significant extent, Washington and New Delhi are united by the challenge of rising Chinese power, which in turn creates conditions for U.S.-India strategic cooperation.[25] The joint statement issued at the end of President Obama's visit to India in January 2015, where he was the first American chief guest at the Republic Day celebrations, asserted that "India's 'Act-East Policy' and the United States' rebalance to Asia provide opportunities for India, the United States, and other Asia-Pacific countries to work closely to strengthen regional ties."[26]

An additional Joint Strategic Vision Statement from the meeting asserted that the two countries "will promote accelerated infrastructure connectivity and economic development in a manner that links South, Southeast and Central Asia."[27] India supports a long-term American presence in Afghanistan, and the New Silk Road vision outlined by the United States coincides with Indian desires for a larger presence in Eurasia. Though the Joint Strategic Vision Statement acknowledged that New Delhi will be working together with Washington in Asia, India has to adapt its policies to the reality of a reduced U.S. footprint in Afghanistan and Central Asia, or to new regional initiatives by China and Russia as well as the reentry of Iran as a full-fledged economic player in Eurasia.

---

22. C. Raja Mohan, "Modi's American Engagement," *Seminar*, no. 668 (April 2015), http://www.india-seminar.com/2015/668/668_c_raja_mohan.htm.

23. Chintamani Mahapatra, "India-US Ties: Reviewing the Relationship" *Strategic Analysis* 39, no. 2 (2015): 170–175.

24. Indian Ministry of External Affairs (MEA), "India-US Relations," December 2014, http://www.mea.gov.in/Portal/ForeignRelation/USA_Dec2014.pdf.

25. Ashley J. Tellis, *Unity in Difference: Overcoming the U.S.-India Divide* (Washington, DC: Carnegie Endowment for International Peace, 2015), http://carnegieendowment.org/files/unity_in_difference.pdf; Brahma Chellaney, "China Pushes Natural Allies India, Japan Closer to US," *Sunday Guardian*, May 30, 2010, http://www.sunday-guardian.com/analysis/china-pushes-natural-allies-india-japan-closer-to-us.

26. Indian MEA, "Joint Statement during the Visit of President of USA to India," January 25, 2015, http://goo.gl/mUbSaE.

27. Indian MEA, "US-India Joint Strategic Vision for the Asia-Pacific and Indian Ocean Region," January 25, 2015, http://goo.gl/HP4db3.

CENTRAL ASIA AND THE SOUTH CAUCASUS

India has good political relations with the eight countries of Central Asia and the Caucasus. These ties are further strengthened through high-level visits, development cooperation, military agreements, and academic and cultural exchanges.[28]

New Delhi has signed strategic partnership agreements with Kazakhstan (2009), Uzbekistan (2011), and Tajikistan (2012).

Tajikistan is India's closest Central Asian neighbor. Dushanbe's proximity and its interdependence with Afghanistan make Tajikistan strategic for India. Starting in the 1990s, India and Tajikistan worked together to support the Northern Alliance in Afghanistan. Tajikistan also hosted a military facility set up by the Indian army at the Farkhor airfield until 2002 to support Northern Alliance fighters.

In 2012, Tajik president Emomali Rahmon visited India and signed six agreements concerning cooperation in the textile industry, health, and medicine, as well as educational and cultural exchanges. Tajik Air soon thereafter resumed direct air links between New Delhi and Dushanbe. The two countries agreed to deepen counterterrorism cooperation and elevate relations to a "strategic partnership." Modi then visited Tajikistan in July 2015, emphasizing defense and counterterrorism cooperation as well as connectivity.

There have been rumors that Indian forces would be deployed to Tajikistan's Ayni airbase, which have been neither confirmed nor denied by either government. India already spent $70 million upgrading the runway and building a control tower, hangars, and other facilities at Ayni.[29] Although there is no significant Indian military presence at the moment, Ayni could prove valuable in the event of an emergency situation in Afghanistan.

New Delhi also regards Uzbekistan as an important partner. The two countries are bound by historical ties as well; Babur, founder of India's Mughal dynasty, came from modern-day Uzbekistan. During his visit to Tashkent in July 2015, Modi emphasized that a strong strategic partnership between India and Uzbekistan is a key pillar of India's engagement with the region. He asked Uzbekistan to consider becoming a member of the INSTC and fast-tracking a uranium export agreement. During the meeting, Uzbek president Islam Karimov asserted that strengthening relations with India is one of Uzbekistan's top foreign policy priorities.[30] The two leaders agreed to boost cooperation in fighting terrorism and in the fields of defense and cybersecurity, including through a bilateral Joint Working Group on Counterterrorism.

Kazakhstan is India's largest trading partner in Central Asia. It exports uranium to India and could provide more investment opportunities in the energy sector. A strategic partnership was signed in 2009 when Kazakh president Nursultan Nazarbayev visited India as a chief guest for India's

---

28. For details, see bilateral country briefs prepared by the Indian MEA, available at http://www.mea.gov.in/.

29. Sandeep Unnithan, "India Wants to Expand Footprint in Central Asia: Modi to Ask Tajikistan for Lease of Ex-Soviet Airbase," *Daily Mail India*, July 11, 2015, http://goo.gl/ECTxBM.

30. Indian MEA, "Joint Statement between Uzbekistan and India during the Prime Minister's visit to Uzbekistan," July 6, 2015, http://goo.gl/cTLrQu.

Republic Day celebrations. During Prime Minister Modi's visit to Astana in July 2015, five agreements were signed including agreements on defense, military-technical cooperation, and uranium purchase.

India and Kazakhstan are also planning to develop freight traffic from western Indian ports to Kazakhstan via Iran. Kazakhstan Railways (KTZ) and India's Adani ports are aiming to construct a terminal at the Mundra port to provide maritime services to Iran's Bandar Abbas port. This line will also connect to the recently inaugurated Iran-Turkmenistan-Kazakhstan railway line.

With Turkmenistan, a significant partnership could develop through the Turkmenistan-Afghanistan-Pakistan-India (TAPI) gas pipeline (discussed below). India, however is exploring multiple options, including the possibility of a new land-sea route through Iran.[31] New Delhi has also started initiatives to invest in downstream industries in Turkmenistan, including petrochemicals and fertilizer. A defense cooperation agreement was also signed during Modi's recent visit to Ashgabat.

Kyrgyzstan's transition to parliamentary democracy was appreciated by New Delhi. Bishkek is keen to learn from India's experiences as a democratic state in the region, and India's Election Commission has agreed to cooperate. New Delhi and Bishkek also maintain an ongoing program of defense cooperation. In 2015 special forces from the two countries conducted a second round of joint exercises termed "Khanjar 2015."

India has also established information technology centers at the Kyrgyz Military Academy and at the Kyrgyz State University in Bishkek. A telemedicine link with India is already operational. To encourage tourism, direct flights between New Delhi and Bishkek have resumed.

If it can position itself as a cost-effective and more efficient alternative to existing Iranian-Russian trans-Caspian shipment within the INSTC, Azerbaijan can emerge as a significant corridor for India-Russia or even India-Europe trade. In the India-Iran-Caspian-Russia route, goods need to be transported via ship, rail, and ship and then back to rail again. It may be more efficient if from Bandar Abbas in Iran goods are transported directly by rail to Russia via Azerbaijan.[32] On the issue of Nagorno-Karabakh, New Delhi supports the territorial integrity and sovereignty of Azerbaijan, and believes that the dispute should be resolved peacefully through dialogue. In 2008, however, India joined Armenia, France, Russia, the United States, and others in voting against the Baku-sponsored UN General Assembly resolution calling for the immediate, complete, and unconditional

---

31. With Iran opening up, India is also looking at a possible undersea pipeline to bring gas from Iran and Oman to India. The proposed pipeline will start from Chabahar in Iran and Ras Al Jafan on the Oman coast. After traversing the Arabian Sea, the pipeline will come ashore at Porbandar in Gujarat in India. The maximum depth of the pipeline will be 3,450 meters and its length will be 1,200–1,300 kilometers. The estimated cost of the project is $4.5 billion, and the pipeline can be built in two years. The pipeline could also be used to bring gas from Turkmenistan to India through a swap arrangement with Iran. For details, see South Asia Gas Enterprise (SAGE), "Middle East to India: Deepwater Gas Pipeline," n.d., http://www.sage-india.com/.

32. Andrew Korybko, "Azerbaijan is the key to unlocking Russian-Indian trade," *Oriental Review*, February 24, 2015, http://orientalreview.org/2015/02/24/azerbaijan-is-the-key-to-unlocking-russian-indian-trade/.

withdrawal of Armenian forces from all the occupied territories of Azerbaijan. Despite this setback, bilateral ties have improved significantly in the last few years.

India's ties with both Armenia and Georgia are cordial. A number of Armenians settled in India during the Mughal emperor Akbar's time. Although some of India's major companies like Tata Power are engaged in big international projects in Georgia, New Delhi has yet to open an embassy in Tbilisi.

03

India in a Reconnecting Eurasia

The transformation from the USSR's centrally planned economy to versions of a market economy in much of post-Soviet Eurasia coincided with reforms aimed at liberalizing India's highly controlled mixed market economy. After a period of slow and negative growth, almost all the Central Asian and South Caucasus economies have grown at a respectable rate since 2000. This growth resulted primarily from high commodity prices, as well as reasonable infrastructure and human capital. The growth momentum provided confidence to the leadership in some of the countries to push for much-needed economic reforms. As a result of this combination of factors, regional economic growth has been impressive since the late 1990s. Until recently, growth was also quite respectable even in Afghanistan, particularly due to reconstruction work implemented through international assistance. These factors created excellent opportunities for India and the Eurasian region to create new economic linkages for mutual benefit.

As discussed earlier, India has been able to forge fruitful economic linkages with many Asian partners. In the last three decades, there has been rapid growth in trade and economic linkages with Southeast Asia and East Asia. Earlier studies revealed that India's qualitative and quantitative engagement with the Asian economies is far deeper than commonly perceived.[1] New Delhi's economic ties with West Asian countries have been traditionally quite strong, and more so now due to energy imports, the diaspora of 2.5 million Indians, and good trade relations.

In an evolving Asian economic architecture, however, India will not be able to play its full potential role if its relations with the Central Asian region and Pakistan remain marginal. As a result, there New Delhi has attempted to develop an economic policy framework for Eurasia that would allow the whole region, including Pakistan and Afghanistan, to be integrated in a mutually beneficial partnership. This framework will also improve India's energy security, as India may finally gain

---

1. See Jairam Ramesh, "India's Economic Integration with Asia" (speech at the Seminar Series on Regional Economic Integration, Asian Development Bank, Manila, November 24, 2008), http://www.icainstitute.org/documents /rameshlecture_India_Economic_Integration.pdf; Mukul G. Asher, *India's Rising Role in Asia*, Discussion Paper No. 121 (New Delhi: RIS, 2007), http://ris.org.in/images/RIS_images/pdf/dp121_pap.pdf.

access to some of the energy resources in the Eurasian region. It also has the potential to funda-mentally reorient India's sea-based continental trade. Simultaneously, it can generate tremendous opportunities for Pakistan, Afghanistan, and the Central Asian region. Indian companies could find tremendous investment opportunities in Central Asia, which in turn can transform their small and medium industries as well as agriculture. The growing realization of these opportunities has influ-enced policymakers not just in India but also in the entire region including Pakistan and Afghanistan.

Many developments, namely, Afghanistan's membership in the South Asian Association for Re-gional Cooperation (SAARC), signing of the South Asian Free Trade Area (SAFTA), RECCA, planned Indian and Pakistani entry into the SCO, improvement in Iran-U.S. relations, groundbreaking on the TAPI gas pipeline, and renewed interest in the Iran-Pakistan-India (IPI) gas pipeline, have provided enough inputs to Indian policymakers to shape their evolving "Look West" policy. This approach echoes New Delhi's very successful "Look East" policy announced in the early 1990s, which radi-cally improved India's ties with East and Southeast Asia. Many analysts promoting the "Look West" policy have concentrated on the West Asian (Middle East) region. But such a policy would also require improving ties with Pakistan, Afghanistan, Central Asia, and the Middle East. Since the combining of Central and South Asia into a single bureau in the State Department, linking these two regions has also been a declared U.S. foreign policy objective. This fits well within emerging India-U.S. ties and adds a new dimension to India–Central Asia relations.

TRADE AND TRANSIT POSSIBILITIES

At present, India's trade with Central Asia and the Caucasus is rather limited (see Table 3.1). Yet with the appropriate framework, this region has the potential to alter the nature and character of India's continental trade. If one looks just beyond Central Asia and the Caucasus toward a wider region encompassing Pakistan, Afghanistan, Iran, Central Asia, the other post-Soviet countries, and Eu-rope, India's trade is very significant. In 2011–2012, India's total trade with these countries amounted to over $180 billion. As a result of overall economic decline, it came down to about $157 billion in 2014–2015 (see Table 3.2). Just before the global economic crisis of 2008–2009, India's trade with this wider region was growing very fast, particularly with Afghanistan, Pakistan, and Iran. If the earlier trend would have continued, it would have climbed to about $400 billion by now.[2] Even after taking into consideration all the cyclical factors and slowdown in exports to the region, trade volume of $250 billion with this broader region is achievable within a limited time.

The majority of Indian trade is presently conducted by sea. Overland India-Pakistan trade has improved in the last 10 years but is mainly limited to bilateral trade, with little reexported to third

---

2. For details, see Gulshan Sachdeva, "Regional Economic Linkages," in *Reconnecting India and Central Asia: Emerging Security and Economic Dimensions*, ed. Nirmala Joshi (Washington, DC: Central Asia–Caucasus Institute & Silk Road Studies Program, 2010), 115–179, http://www.silkroadstudies.org/resources/pdf/Monographs/2010_03_MONO_Joshi _India-Central-Asia.pdf.

countries.[3] Border trade with China was stopped after the 1962 India-China war, though a limited opening has been made through the Nathula Pass in recent years. If the general state of the political economy in the region improves and even if about 20 percent of total trade is conducted by road, at least $50 billion of Indian trade could pass through Afghanistan and the Central Asian region annually within a few years.

CENTRAL ASIA AND THE SOUTH CAUCASUS

At the time of the Soviet Union, Indian economic contacts with the republics of the USSR were all through Moscow. The nature and character of Indo-Soviet trade and economic relations largely determined relations with the Eurasian region as a whole. India was able to build a special trade relationship with the Soviet bloc in which trade was carried out in local, nonconvertible currencies. Although this arrangement had many usual weaknesses like corruption, patronage, and transactions in low-quality products, it helped many small and medium-size private Indian companies to become exporters.

After the disintegration of the Soviet Union, this artificial trading relationship suddenly disappeared. As a result, economic relations with the region declined considerably.[4] In the last few years, however, there has been an upward trend. Currently, the Indian official two-way annual trade with Central Asia and the Caucasus region is about $2 billion annually, half of which is with Kazakhstan. Additionally, Azerbaijan is becoming a significant trading partner. Apart from these countries, India's economic relations with other countries in the region are minimal. The main commodities being exported from India to the region are pharmaceuticals, tea, ready-made garments, meat products, leather goods, jute products, cosmetics, cotton yarn, machinery, machine tools, rice, plastic products, machinery and instruments, electronic goods, and chemicals. Imports from the region are largely restricted to petroleum products, zinc, fertilizer, iodine, raw cotton, and iron and steel.[5]

INVESTMENT OPPORTUNITIES FOR INDIAN COMPANIES

The countries of Central Asia and the South Caucasus provide good investment opportunities for Indian business. This is clearly shown by London-based Indian steel tycoon Laxmi Mittal. His company, ArcelorMittal Temirtau, is the largest producer in Kazakhstan's steel and mining sector. The company's integrated steel plant located in Temirtau has an annual capacity of 4 million tons of crude steel. The company also operates eight coal mines across the Karaganda region and four

3. Nisha Taneja and Sanjib Pohit, eds., *India-Pakistan Trade: Strengthening Economic Relations* (New Delhi: Springer, 2015).

4. Gulshan Sachdeva, "India-Russia Economic Relations: Gradual Shift from State Dominant Linkages to Private Initiatives," in *Globalisation in China, India and Russia: Emergence of National Groups and Global Strategies of Firms,* ed. Jean-François Huchet, Xavier Richet, and Joël Ruet (New Delhi: Academic Foundation, 2007), 217–239.

5. Sachdeva, "Regional Economic Linkages."

Table 3.1. India's Trade with Central Asia and the South Caucasus, 2010–2011 to 2014–2015 (million USD)

	2010–11	2011–12	2012–13	2013–14	2014–15
Central Asia					
Kazakhstan	310	436	426	918	952
Kyrgyzstan	27	31	37	35	39
Tajikistan	41	30	48	55	58
Turkmenistan	36	63	78	88	106
Uzbekistan	81	126	157	146	226
Caucasus					
Armenia	27	44	42	74	92
Azerbaijan	242	747	608	1261	309
Georgia	111	181	182	115	105
Total Indian Trade	**619,585**	**795,283**	**791,137**	**764,605**	**758,371**

Source: Department of Commerce, Ministry of Commerce and Industry, Government of India.

iron ore mines in Karaganda, Akmola, and Kostanay oblasts.[6] The company is, however, facing difficulties due to the increase of Russian imports to Kazakhstan resulting from the devaluated ruble and reduced barriers to trade with Russia in the context of the EAEU.

Over the past decade, New Delhi has created a new institutional apparatus to facilitate trade and investment with this region. During this time, the Indian government set up bilateral intergovernmental commissions for trade and economic, scientific, and technical cooperation with all eight Central Asian and South Caucasus countries, which have been meeting on a regular basis. Relations are further institutionalized through joint working groups in various fields, namely, information technology, science and technology, hydrocarbons, military-technical cooperation, and others. The Indian government also extends small lines of credit for the countries in the region to

6. See ArcelorMittal, "ArcelorMittal in Kazakhstan," n.d., http://aktau.arcelormittal.com/who-we-are/arcelormittal -kazakhstan.aspx?sc_lang=en.

Table 3.2. India's Trade with Europe, Central Asia, Other CIS Countries, Afghanistan, Iran, and Pakistan, 2007–2008 to 2014–2015 (million USD)

	2007–08	2008–09	2009–10	2010–11	2011–12	2012–13	2013–14	2014–15
Exports								
European Union	34,535	39,351	36,028	46,039	52,556	50,422	51,581	49,315
Rest of Europe	2,752	2,724	2,494	3,847	5,195	5,580	6,690	6,946
5 Central Asian Republics	232	258	269	302	430	551	538	605
Other CIS Countries	1,508	1,666	1,418	2,378	2,630	3,131	2,954	2,791
Afghanistan	249	395	463	422	511	473	474	423
Iran	1,943	2,534	1,853	2,792	2,411	3,351	4,971	4,175
Pakistan	1,950	1,439	1,573	2,039	1,541	2,065	2,274	1,857
Total	43,169	48,366	44,098	57,819	65,274	65,573	69,482	66,112
Imports								
European Union	38,450	42,733	38,433	44,539	56,871	52,275	49,950	49,207
Rest of Europe	13,127	14,528	17,279	26,640	36,838	35,254	21,059	24,712

5 Central Asian Republics	112	260	212	193	258	195	703	776
Other CIS Countries	3,675	6,367	5,891	5,471	8,146	7,685	7,019	6,890
Afghanistan	109	126	125	146	132	160	209	262
Iran	10,943	12,376	11,540	10,928	13,790	11,594	10,307	8,955
Pakistan	287	370	275	332	398	542	427	497
Total	66,703	76,760	73,755	88,249	116,433	107,705	89,674	91,299
Total Trade								
European Union	73,075	82,084	74,461	91,358	109,427	102,697	101,531	98,522
Rest of Europe	15,879	17,252	19,763	30,479	42,033	40,834	27,749	31,658
5 Central Asian Republics	344	518	481	486	688	746	1,241	1,381
Other CIS Countries	5,183	5,183	8,033	8,040	10,776	10,816	9,973	9,681
Afghanistan	359	520	588	557	643	633	683	685
Iran	12,887	14,910	13,394	13,670	16,201	14,945	15,278	13,130
Pakistan	2,238	1,810	1,849	2,666	1,939	2,607	2,701	2,354
Total	**109,965**	**125,127**	**117,845**	**146,068**	**181,707**	**173,278**	**159,156**	**157,411**

Source: Author's calculations based on data from Department of Commerce, Ministry of Commerce and Industry, Government of India.

Table 3.3. MOUs Signed by FICCI with Counterpart Organizations in Eurasia

Country	Counterpart Organization
Armenia	Union of Manufacturers and Businessmen (Employers) of Armenia
Kazakhstan	Kazakhstan Chamber of Commerce and Industry
Kyrgyzstan	Chamber of Commerce and Industry of Kyrgyz Republic
Tajikistan	Chamber of Commerce and Industry of the Republic of Tajikistan
Uzbekistan	Chamber of Commodity Producers and Entrepreneurs of Uzbekistan

enable Indian firms to export to these markets without repayment risk.[7] New Delhi has also signed double taxation avoidance agreements with these states, and Indian banks have interbanking arrangements with countries in the region.

New Delhi has also signed many agreements with the countries of post-Soviet Eurasia for technical economic cooperation under the Indian Technical and Economic Cooperation (ITEC) program. This is a large training and capacity-building program run by the Indian government through the Ministry of External Affairs (MEA) since 1964. Every year more than 10,000 (about 8,500 civilian and about 1,500 defense) personnel from more than 150 friendly countries are trained in 47 different institutions in India.[8] So far thousands of candidates from the Eurasian region have come to India under the program in various disciplines, such as diplomacy, banking, finance, trade, management, and small business promotion. In 2014–2015, 420 training slots were allocated to Central Asia, including about 150 each to Tajikistan and Uzbekistan, 85 to Kyrgyzstan, and 20 to Turkmenistan. Armenia and Georgia were allocated 20 and 15 slots, respectively. In addition to the ITEC, the Indian Council of Cultural Relations (ICCR) also offers fellowships to students from mainly developing countries to study in Indian universities. In 2014–2015 about 100 fellowships were given to students from the five Central Asian republics. The Federation of Indian Chambers of Commerce and Industry (FICCI) has set up joint business councils with Kazakhstan, Uzbekistan, and the Kyrgyz republic. It has also signed memoranda of understanding (MOUs) with numerous counterpart organizations in the region (see Table 3.3).

The India-CIS Chamber of Commerce, the Confederation of Indian Industry (CII), and the Associated Chambers of Commerce and Industry of India (ASSOCHAM) are also active in the region. The

---

7. Under this scheme, around 15 to 20 percent of the contract's value is paid in advance by the importers, and the balance of the contract value is disbursed by the Indian EXIM Bank to the exporters on shipment of goods. The recovery of credit extended to the overseas buyer is taken care of by the EXIM Bank, without recourse to the Indian exporter.

8. See ITEC, "About ITEC," n.d., http://itec.mea.gov.in/?1320?000.

CII is focused more on Kazakhstan. The ASSOCHAM has recently signed an MOU with East Kazakhstan Oblast.

Many Indian business organizations and think tanks have identified areas of cooperation, like energy, food processing, textiles, tourism, information technology, education, consultancy services, petrochemicals, and construction.[9]

Another area of major interest to Indian businesses would be to participate in the continuing privatization process in the region. India's Spentex Industries acquired Tashkent-To'yetpa Tekstil, a state-owned spinning company in Uzbekistan for $81 million in 2006. In 2007, Uzbekistan also announced many incentives to attract Indian textile companies. Uzbekistan and Kazakhstan are heavily marketing a bounty of fiscal sops to Indian textile firms.[10] India's Punj Lloyd has also participated in oil pipeline projects in Kazakhstan.[11] The experience of Spentex in Uzbekistan, however, was disappointing, and it filed for bankruptcy in 2012 losing about $100 million. India's Tata Power is involved in construction and operation of the $404 million Shuakhevi hydropower plant in Georgia as a joint venture with Norway's Clean Energy Invest (40 percent each) and the International Financial Corporation (IFC) (20 percent). The project is being financed by the IFC, the Asian Development Bank (ADB), and the European Bank for Reconstruction and Development (EBRD), and is expected to produce about 450 gigawatt hours of power annually. It will meet Georgia's electricity demand during winter and export electricity to Turkey during other times. It is also the first hydropower project in Georgia that is certified by the UN Framework Convention on Climate Change for carbon emission reductions.[12] If some of the Central Asian countries are able to reform their land policies, there is a tremendous possibility of investment in the agricultural sector.

The Export-Import Bank of India (EXIM Bank) has also started a trade promotion program for the region called "Focus CIS Program." Under the program, it "operates a comprehensive range of financing, advisory and support programs to promote and facilitate India's trade and investment with the CIS countries." It extends lines of credit to these countries and has assisted many Indian companies to secure contracts in mining, energy, and transportation, and helped them in projects funded by multilateral institutions. The bank has also supported Indian firms setting up joint ventures in the pharma sector in Kazakhstan, Uzbekistan, and Ukraine. It has forged alliances with UZBEKINVEST, the National Export Import Insurance Company of Uzbekistan, and the National Bank for Foreign Economic Activity of Uzbekistan, among others. A consultancy company promoted by the EXIM Bank called Global Procurement Consultants Limited has taken a number of projects in Armenia, Georgia, Kyrgyzstan, and Uzbekistan. Another joint venture promoted by the EXIM Bank, Global Trade Finance Limited, offers foreign trade financing products such as forfeiting

9. Ramgopal Agarwala, *Towards Comprehensive Economic Co-operation between India and Central Asian Republics*, Discussion Paper No. 108 (New Delhi: RIS, 2006), http://www.ris.org.in//dp108_pap.pdf; CII, *Central Asia and Indian Business: Emerging Trends and Opportunities* (seminar proceedings, New Delhi: CII, May 2003).

10. "Central Asian Countries Woo Indian Textile Cos," *Hindu Business Line*, January 22, 2007, http://www.thehindubusinessline.com/todays-paper/central-asian-countries-woo-indian-textile-cos/article1647160.ece.

11. For details, see the Punj Lloyd company website, http://www.punjlloyd.com.

12. ADB, "IFC, ADB, EBRD, Tata Power, and Clean Energy Help Georgia Achieve Energy Self-sufficiency" (news release, March 19, 2015), http://goo.gl/W4Ohg4.

Table 3.4. Indian Commercial and Other Contacts in Eurasia

Country	Presence of Indian Firms	Potential Areas for Investment	Indian Community
Armenia	Kalpataru	IT, jewelry & diamonds, mining & metallurgy, agro food processing, tourism, chemical industries	700 (mainly medical students)
Azerbaijan	Lupin Laboratories, Micro Labs, Medicare, Rezlon, Quaramax, Ajanta Pharma	Agro machinery & agro food processing, chemicals, IT, metallurgy & energy industries, machine building industry, telecom., textiles, tourism	800 (two Indian community associations: Indian Association Azerbaijan and Malyalee Association)
Georgia	Tata Power; individual investors mainly from Punjab (around 150) have acquired agricultural land for cultivation	Agriculture farming, hydro power, tourism, manufacturing (textile, elec. tools, mining). agriculture technology & infrastructure	2,000 (of which about 700 are mainly medical students)
Kazakhstan	ONGC Videsh, Punjab National Bank, Bharat Heavy Electricals Limited, Claris Lifesciences, Dr. Reddy's Lab., Mega Lifesciences, KEC International, Sunpharma, Ranbaxy, Alkem Lab, Lupin, Ajanta Pharma	Chemicals, pharmaceuticals, oil & gas, agriculture & food processing, construction, telecommunications, minerals & metals	4,200 (of which 700 are mainly medical students)
Kyrgyzstan		Tourism, agro food processing, mining & metallurgy, hydro power	4,000 (mainly medical students)
Tajikistan	CHL, Ajanta Pharma, Kalpataru, BHEL	Hydro power, light industries	400 (of which 300 are medical students)
Turkmenistan	ONGC Videsh (OVL) is in the process of opening its office	Oil and gas, tourism	534 (mainly in the energy and construction sectors)
Uzbekistan	Global Impex, Nova Pharm, Global Transportation Systems, Lupin, Shreta Lifesciences, Ajanta Pharma, Himalai Company, Dr. Reddy's Lab., Claris Lifesciences, Minda Automotive Solutions	Oil and gas refining, textiles	Small Indian community

Source: FICCI and MEA.

and factoring in Armenia, Azerbaijan, Belarus, Russia, Tajikistan, and Ukraine. The Indian EXIM Bank also maintains relations with corresponding institutions in the region.[13]

Table 3.4 summarizes the Indian commercial and human resource presence in Eurasia and potential areas of investment and cooperation.[14]

One important aspect of India's presence is the large number of Indian students studying in the region, mainly in the field of medicine. During the Soviet period a large number of students were going to various Soviet republics either through government channels or through the Communist Party of India. Currently, these students are mainly paying medical students who have gone to these places because of easier admission and lower costs. These students live there for longer periods, know the local languages, and have developed good personal contacts. As Hari Vasudevan has pointed out, Indian students studying in Soviet universities were one of the main vehicles of commercial contacts between India and Russia in the 1990s when state-to-state linkages had broken down.[15] These students today represent a huge pool of human resources, which could be utilized for improving ties with the region.

ENERGY

Despite fairly low per capita energy consumption, India is the world's fourth-largest energy consumer (after China, the United States, and Russia) and is likely to become the third-largest by 2030. Although India has 18 percent of the global population, it uses only 6 percent of the world's primary energy, though its energy consumption has almost doubled since 2000 and the potential for further growth is high.[16] To catch up with the rest of dynamic Asia and to reduce poverty, India must continue growing at least about 8 to 10 percent in the next two decades. Because India is relatively poor in oil and gas resources, it has to depend on imports to meet its energy supplies. Even though domestic production of energy resources is projected to increase, import dependence will continue at a high level.

The main area of import will be crude oil, where nearly 78 percent of the demand will have to be met from imports by 2017. Import dependence for coal is also estimated to increase from 19 percent in 2011–2012 to 22.4 percent in 2017 and 26 percent 2022. With already about 80 percent of its crude oil requirements met by imports, India's oil import bill was close to $140 billion in 2012–2013. Due to falling oil prices, the oil import bill came down to $124 billion in 2014–2015.

---

13. For details, see Indian Ministry of Commerce and Industry, "Trade Promotion Programme—Focus: CIS," http://commerce.nic.in/trade/international_tpp_cis_8.asp.

14. The list is mainly based on various publications of the FICCI and country briefs provided by the Indian MEA.

15. Hari Vasudevan, *Shadows of Substance: Indo-Russian Trade and Military Technical Cooperation since 1991* (New Delhi: Manohar, 2010).

16. International Energy Agency (IEA), *India Energy Outlook: World Energy Outlook Special Report* (Paris: IEA, 2015), http://www.worldenergyoutlook.org/media/weowebsite/2015/IndiaEnergyOutlook_WEO2015.pdf.

The Indian economy also relies heavily on coal, which accounts for about 70 percent of electricity generation. After China and the United States, India is the world's third-largest coal user. As a result of the government's policy of diversifying the country's energy mix, the share of natural gas has increased to just over 9 percent. Other sources, such as wind, solar, and nuclear power, still account for very small shares. Although coal will still be a very important source of energy, the alternative policy scenario of the government visualizes a reduction in its demand by 2030. In the alternative scenario, coal demand will grow much slower and oil demand will also decrease somewhat due to the introduction of compressed natural gas (CNG) and fuel efficiency. Similarly, the role of nuclear power is envisaged to increase still further. Even if all these changes are implemented, India will still be importing between 29 and 59 percent of its total commercial primary energy by 2030.

According to the U.S. Energy Administration, in 2013, India's sources of crude oil included Saudi Arabia (20 percent), Iraq (14 percent), Iran (6 percent), other Middle East (22 percent), Venezuela (12 percent), other Western Hemisphere (7 percent), Nigeria (8 percent), other Africa (8 percent), and others (3 percent).[17]

Officials believe that India's energy security can be increased by (a) diversifying both the energy mix and the sources of energy imports, (b) seriously pursuing overseas acquisitions of energy assets, and (c) initiating reforms to attract foreign investment as well as improving domestic production, distribution, and consumption.

In the last 10 years, energy diplomacy has also become one of the main agendas of India's foreign and security policy. India is seriously pursuing nuclear energy, as well as imports from sources beyond the Middle East.[18] New energy sources from the Eurasian region are going to play a growing important role in Indian energy strategy in the coming years.

In the early 1990s, there was a lot of discussion about the Caspian region becoming another Middle East. These discussions and projected scenarios have become relatively sober. Still, the region has significant proven global oil and gas reserves. Apart from Russia, Azerbaijan and Kazakhstan could play an important role in diversifying Indian imports. Indian companies are trying hard to get a strong foothold in the region. Indian companies have invested in Russia's Sakhalin1 oil and gas field, and India's state-owned Oil and Natural Gas Corporation (ONGC) purchased British-based Imperial Energy, whose key assets are located in Siberia.

Competition in the region has been tough, though, as China has been pursuing a similar strategy. India and China may be cooperating in other areas, but when it comes to Eurasian energy, competition has been fierce. This was clearly illustrated in late 2005 when China outbid India to acquire PetroKazakhstan, Kazakhstan's third-largest oil producer, with China National Petroleum Corporation (CNPC) eventually raising its bid to $4.18 billion.

---

17. U.S. Energy Information Administration (EIA), "India: International Energy Data and Analysis," June 26, 2014, https://www.eia.gov/beta/international/analysis.cfm?iso=IND.

18. For details, see Gulshan Sachdeva, "Geoeconomics and Energy for India," in *Handbook of India's International Relations*, ed. David Scott (London: Routledge, 2011), 47–56.

After trying for many years, India is slowly getting into the energy sector in the region. Although India's ONGC Videsh Limited (OVL) had been trying to gain a foothold in Kazakhstan since 1995, these efforts got a boost when OVL entered into an MOU with Kazakhstan's state energy company KazMunaiGaz (KMG) in February 2005 for cooperation in the hydrocarbon sector. In April 2011, during the then prime minister Manmohan Singh's visit to Kazakhstan, a final agreement was signed for OVL to take a 25 percent stake in the Satpayev block in Kazakhstan's sector of the Caspian Sea, which holds estimated reserves of 1.8 billion barrels. OVL is investing about $400 million in the project and oil is expected to flow from it by 2020.[19] Drilling of the project was launched during Modi's July 2015 visit to Kazakhstan.[20]

ONGC Videsh also bought a 2.7 percent stake in the Azeri-Chirag-Guneshli (ACG) field in Azerbaijan, along with a 2.4 percent stake in the associated Baku-Tbilisi-Ceyhan (BTC) pipeline for $1 billion.

In 2013, India suffered a setback in its efforts in Kazakhstan. OVL was very close to finalizing a $5 billion deal for the acquisition of an 8.4 percent stake in the North Caspian Sea Production Sharing Agreement that includes the Kashagan field from ConocoPhillips. Though OVL got approval from partners for acquisition of the ConocoPhillips stake, the Kazakh government, using its own legal rights, sold this stake to China's CNPC for a reported sum of $5.2 to 5.4 billion. According to some estimates, India has lost at least $12.5 billion of deals to China in recent years.[21] Recently, there were reports that the ONGC was offered an alternative midsized Abai oil block in Caspian Sea by the Kazakh government. With the declining oil prices, however, ONGC did not find the offer particularly attractive.[22] Overall, Indian oil interests in the Eurasian region are summarized in Table 3.5.

As far as gas imports are concerned, both Turkmenistan and Uzbekistan are important. Both have large amounts of proven gas reserves. Since the mid-1990s, there has been a lot of discussion on the TAPI gas pipeline. The 1,700 km pipeline will run from the South Yolotan (Galkynysh)-Osman fields in Turkmenistan to Afghanistan, and from there it will be constructed alongside the highway running from Herat to Kandahar, and then via Quetta and Multan in Pakistan. The final destination of the pipeline will be to Fazilka in Indian Punjab. The project will be able to transport up to 30 billion cubic meters of natural gas annually from Turkmenistan to South Asian countries. The agreement signed by the countries envisages delivery of 90 million cubic meters per day (mcm/d) of gas from Turkmenistan to participating countries with 38 mcm/d each going to Pakistan and India and 14 mcm/d for Afghanistan. Analysts have pointed out many uncertainties concerning the project. These include uncertain gas reserves in Turkmenistan, the poor security situation in Afghanistan, and strained relations between India and Pakistan.

---

19. For details, see Indian MEA, "Bilateral Agreements Concluded during PM's Visit to Kazakhstan," April 16, 2011, http://mea.gov.in/bilateral-documents.htm?dtl/4845/Bilateral+agreements+concluded+during+PMs+visit+to+Kazakhstan.

20. "PM Narendra Modi Launches OVL Oil Block Project in Kazakhstan," *Economic Times*, July 7, 2015, http://goo.gl/iJEyWs.

21. "India Loses $5 bn Bid for Kashagan Oil Field to China," *Economic Times*, July 2, 2013, http://goo.gl/ADZXcr.

22. "India Rejects Kazakhstan's Offer for Abai Oilfield," *Economic Times*, June 17, 2015, http://goo.gl/7JtZqz.

Table 3.5. Indian Energy Interests in Eurasia

Country	Name of Block	Participating Interest and Details of Other Partners
Russia	Sakhalin 1	ONGC Videsh (20%)
		Exxon Neftegas (operator, 30%)
		SODECO (Japan, 30%)
		Subsidiaries of Rosneft (20%)
	Imperial Energy	ONGC Videsh (100%)
	License 61	Oil India Limited (joint operator, 50%)
		PetroNeft (joint operator, 50%)
Kazakhstan	Satpayev	ONGC Videsh (25%)
		KazMunaiGaz (KMG, operator, 75%)
Azerbaijan	Azeri Chirag Guneshli	ONGC Videsh (2.72%)
		BP (operator, 36%)
		SOCAR (12%)
		Chevron (11%)
		INPEX (11%)
		Statoil (9%)
		Exxon (9%)
		TPAO (97%)
		Itochu (4%)
	BTC Pipeline (1,760 km)	ONGC Videsh (2.36%)
		BP (operator, 30%)
		SOCAR (25%)
		Statoil (8.7%)
		TPAO (6.53%)
		Itochu (3.4%)
		INPEX (2.5%)
		ENI (5%)
		Total (5%)
		Conoco Phillips (2.5%)

Source: ONGC website and Annual Reports of the Ministry of Petroleum and Gas, Government of India.

India was formally invited to join the TAPI project in 2006. In the last few years, the four countries involved in the project have signed most of the intergovernmental agreements required for its commencement. A broad agreement on transit fee was also agreed upon.[23] To accelerate the project, parties formed a ministerial-level steering committee and technical working group.

While the ADB was appointed as the transaction adviser, the search for a consortium leader continued.[24] Starting with Bridas, Unocal, and Delta during the Taliban regime in the 1990s, many energy giants such as Chevron, Exxon, and BP showed interest in the project. More recently, Total of France and Dubai-based Dragon Oil were in discussion with the Turkmen government. None of them, however, committed to the project either due to security and financial considerations or due to the reluctance of the Turkmen government to sign a production-sharing agreement for onshore blocks with foreign companies. As a result, the four countries agreed on a consortium composed of their respective national oil companies, with Turkmengaz, the national oil company of Turkmenistan, as the consortium leader. This obviously is not the best arrangement, as none of the national companies have experience of building a pipeline of this magnitude. To reflect new realities, the participating countries will also perhaps renegotiate gas price agreements reached earlier.[25] Still, it shows the political commitment of partner countries in going ahead with the project despite the evident difficulties. The countries hope that these developments may encourage some companies to join the project at a later stage. At least the project has cleared political hurdles and gone to the very first stage of implementation. Leaders from the four countries participated in a groundbreaking ceremony in Mary, Turkmenistan, in December 2015. To some extent, the event defied skeptics who have always considered TAPI's relevance limited only to academic and diplomatic conferences. Indian vice president Hamid Ansari, who represented India at the groundbreaking event in Mary, rightly called it "more than a project" and "first steps towards unification of the region."

Turkmenistan, Afghanistan, and Pakistan also signed an MOU for a power transmission line. The line will be constructed parallel to the TAPI gas pipeline. Also, there are plans to connect the four countries by a parallel fiber optic cable. For this reason Afghan president Ghani called it a "super highway of cooperation and coordination that will connect again South Asia and Central Asia together."

The strategic significance of the project is potentially huge. Once completed, the TAPI can become a game changer in regional geopolitics and a promoter of regional economic integration. Due to the significant transit revenues it would generate for Afghanistan, it also has the potential to lessen that country's economic difficulties in the coming years. If the project is completed successfully, it could bring together the Indian Connect Central Asia policy and the China-Pakistan Economic Corridor (CPEC) of the Chinese OBOR project.

---

23. India and Pakistan agreed on the principle of a "Uniform Transit Fee." Basically, it meant that Pakistan will accept whatever transit fee India and Afghanistan agree upon. Later, the Indian government approved the payment of 50 cents per million metric British thermal units as the transit fee to Pakistan and Afghanistan.

24. For details see Gulshan Sachdeva, "TAPI: Time for the Big Push," *Central Asia–Caucasus Analyst* 15, no. 14 (July 13, 2013), http://www.cacianalyst.org/publications/analytical-articles/item/12772-tapi-time-for-the-big-push.html.

25. "India to Renegotiate TAPI Gas Prices," *Economic Times*, November 9, 2015, http://goo.gl/E9PSKE.

Due to the Chinese slowdown and decline in Russian gas purchases, the dynamics of the Central Asian gas market are changing significantly. Turkmenistan presently exports gas to China, Russia, and Iran. Both Russia and Iran have reduced their imports. Russia was mostly reexporting Turkmen gas to Europe. With both prices and demand in Europe falling, the long-term contract that it signed with Turkmenistan is becoming unprofitable. When renegotiations did not work, Moscow unilaterally reduced imports. After the lifting of international sanctions, Iran is also likely to build its domestic and export infrastructure and reduce imports from Turkmenistan.

In response, China has already become the largest export market for Turkmen gas, with some in Ashgabat now worried about overdependence on the Chinese market and seeking alternatives, including in South Asia. If TAPI becomes a reality, it will also encourage Russia to plan sending hydrocarbons to South Asia by pipelines. Already India and Russia have set up a working group to explore the possibility of bringing Russian hydrocarbons to India either via the Afghanistan-Pakistan route or via China.

Earlier, the Gas Authority of India (GAIL) had signed an MOU with Uzbekneftegaz (UNG) for oil and gas exploration and production in Uzbekistan. GAIL had also agreed to set up a few liquefied petroleum gas (LPG) plants in western Uzbekistan along with UNG. Capital investment in each LPG plant will reportedly be $50–60 million. These plants will produce LPG predominantly for the domestic market in Uzbekistan.[26] In 2011, ONGC Videsh also signed an MOU with UNG for joint cooperation in the upstream exploration and production (E&P) in Uzbekistan as well as in third countries.[27] India and Uzbekistan are also cooperating in Afghanistan, where Uzbekistan is supplying electricity through a power transmission line built by India.

Uranium purchases from the region are also becoming an important area of cooperation. As Kazakhstan has large reserves of uranium, India is keen to import it for its growing nuclear industry. In 2011, Kazakhstan agreed to supply 2,100 tons of uranium to India's nuclear plants by 2014.[28] During Prime Minister Modi's visit to Astana in 2015, Kazakhstan agreed to supply a further 5,000 tons of uranium for the period 2015–2019.[29] Similarly, in 2014, the state-owned Uzbek mining firm NMMC (Navoi Mining and Metallurgy Combine) agreed to supply 2,000 metric tons of uranium ore concentrate to India for the period between 2014 and 2018.[30]

LINKAGES WITH EURASIA THROUGH REGIONAL ORGANIZATIONS AND INITIATIVES

Until about a decade ago, India used a cautious approach to regionalism, and was engaged in only a few bilateral or regional initiatives, mainly through preferential trade agreements (PTAs) or

26. "GAIL to Set up LPG Plants in Uzbekistan," *Hindu Business Line*, May 2, 2006, http://goo.gl/OfIJDw.

27. "ONGC Videsh Inks Pact with Uzbek Firm," *Business Standard*, May 18, 2011, http://goo.gl/6ku3co.

28. "Kazakhstan to Supply 2100 Tonnes Uranium by 2014," *DNA*, April 16, 2011, http://goo.gl/ZyF9wd.

29. P. Stobdan, "India and Central Asia: Untying the Energy Knot" *Strategic Analysis* 40, no. 1 (2016): 14–25.

30. "India Widens N-fuel Base, Signs up Uzbek Firm for Uranium Supplies," *Indian Express*, August 27, 2014, http://goo.gl/1pr9ql.

through open regionalism. The collapse of the Doha Round of World Trade Organization (WTO) negotiations pushed many countries, including India, to look for alternatives to multilateral negotiations to improve their trade positions. India put its regional trade agreements on the fast track. As explained earlier, it has concluded comprehensive economic cooperation agreements (CECAs) with many countries. These CECAs establish FTAs in goods (a zero customs duty regime within a fixed time frame on items covering substantial trade, and a relatively small negative list of sensitive items with none or limited-duty concessions), services, and investment and identified areas of economic cooperation. Many of these agreements are with Asian countries.

Compared with these broader trends, India's links with the Eurasian region have been relatively weak despite the fact that most Central Asian and Caucasus countries are members of a wide range of regional groupings. Knowing that it does not have direct access to Eurasia, along with its difficult relations with Pakistan, India's major initiative in the 1990s was cooperation in building a new trade and transit corridor. Russia, Iran, and India are founding members of the INSTC (see Map 3.1). Many other countries have joined the project, which provides a shorter route for trade to Iran, Russia, and countries in Eurasia. There are many sectors, but for India the corridor facilitates movement of goods via Iran, the Caspian Sea, and Astrakhan to Russia and adjoining countries, including Central Asia.

The main transport project being undertaken in this program with Indian involvement is the development of a new port complex at Chabahar on the coast of Iran, from where a road goes north to the border with Afghanistan. It is 72 km from Pakistan's deep-sea Gwadar port, built with the Chinese assistance, and closer to India than Iran's existing port at Bandar Abbas. In the last decade Chabahar faced many delays, but now it seems that both the Indian and Iranian governments have agreed to accelerate the project.[31] An agreement to this effect was signed in December 2015 by the Indian foreign minister. Per the agreement, India will offer Iran a credit line, invest in the country's petrochemical sector and downstream oil industry, and participate in the construction of a Chabahar-Zahedan railroad.[32] There were also reports that India was planning to construct a 900 km railway line that will connect the Chabahar port with the Hajigak region of Afghanistan, where Indian companies were awarded iron ore projects.[33] India has also completed the construction of a 218 km link from Zaranj on the Iran-Afghan border to Delaram from where all major cities in Afghanistan and the Central Asian republics are connected. India has also built the Afghan side of the 22 km Zaranj-Milak road. Another road transport project involves a Chabahar-Faraj-Bam railway project, which connects the port to Central Asia and Europe by rail.[34] The Chabahar port is

---

31. In October 2104, New Delhi agreed that an Indian joint venture company will lease two fully constructed berths in the Chabahar port's Phase I project for a period of 10 years, which could be renewed. It was also agreed that the company will invest $85 million for equipping the two berths. See Indian Press Information Bureau, "India's participation in the development of Chahbahar port in Iran" (press release, October 18, 2014), http://pib.nic.in/newsite/PrintRelease.aspx?relid=110685.

32. "Iran, India Ink Economic Co-op Agreement, Chabahar Port in Focus," *Tehran Times*, December 30, 2015, http://www.tehrantimes.com/index_View.asp?code=251862.

33. "India's Track 3: Afghan-Iran Rail link," *Hindustan Times*, November 1, 2011, http://goo.gl/ZXu4Gv.

34. For details, see Mohiuddin Alamgir, *Report on the Economic Impact of Central-South Asian Road Corridors* (paper from the Central and South Asia Transport and Trade Forum [CSATTF], Second Ministerial Conference, December 2005); Roy, "Iran," 957–975.

Map 3.1. International North-South Trade Corridor and Alternative Routes

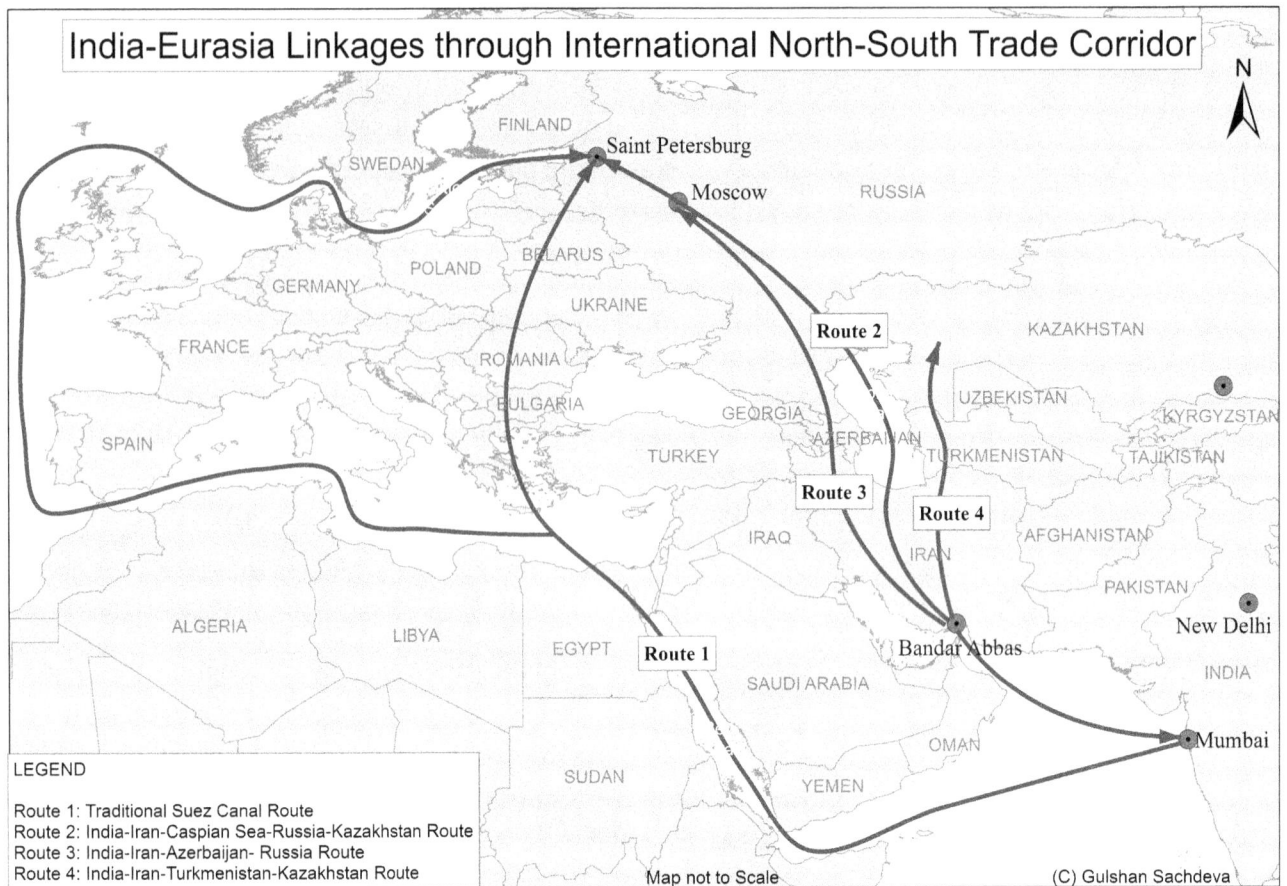

India-Eurasia Linkages through International North-South Trade Corridor

N

LEGEND

Route 1: Traditional Suez Canal Route
Route 2: India-Iran-Caspian Sea-Russia-Kazakhstan Route
Route 3: India-Iran-Azerbaijan- Russia Route
Route 4: India-Iran-Turkmenistan-Kazakhstan Route

Map not to Scale

(C) Gulshan Sachdeva

strategically important for India, as it serves as the entry point for India's outreach into Afghanistan and Eurasia, bypassing Pakistan. The port could also become important to the U.S. logistics in the region, if in the future some working relationship is developed between Iran and the United States.

Although the INSTC was an ambitious project, it really did not take off earlier. One the main reasons is the low volume of India-Russia trade, which was supposed to provide major traffic. In the absence of large volumes, shipping companies still prefer their original routes with established logistics. Although Iranian ports work efficiently, Indian exporters to Central Asia preferred using the Chinese port of Qingdao, which was 35 percent cheaper than the Iranian route, although transit time was longer compared with Bandar Abbas.[35] In the last few years, some companies have started using Iranian ports.

Until recently, India was not really connected with Central Asia through any regional organization. This may change with India's impending membership in the SCO, which would thereby become the first organization formally linking Central and South Asia. Since its formation India was not quite sure what priority this organization deserved. It provided China, Russia, and the Central Asian states a delicate equilibrium in the new geopolitical situation. India was never featured in this

---

35. Jyotsna Dube Choudhri, "An Insight of CIS" (mimeo, paper presented at "Silk Road and India: Historical and Contemporary Relevance" conference, New Delhi, December 27–28, 2011).

equilibrium, though Central Asians perceived India's potential to play a balancing role.[36] In the beginning, India showed interest in the SCO, but the impression is that China never really wanted India in the grouping. India was welcomed as an observer in SCO only when China was also admitted in the SAARC as an observer. With growing uncertainty about Afghanistan, where the SCO may play some role in the future, India decided to finally ask for membership in 2012. At the Ufa summit in 2015, it was finally agreed that India and Pakistan will be admitted as full members in 2016 when all formalities are completed.[37] There are reports that the organization is also considering Iran's application for membership once UN sanctions are lifted.[38]

For China, the SCO now could play a larger role in the OBOR project. Beijing recently proposed that the SCO will establish six platforms for cooperation in areas including security, production capacity, connectivity, financial cooperation, regional trade cooperation, and cooperation on social affairs.[39] At this point, no one has any clear idea whether China and the SCO can bring anything new to the table regarding the transition in Afghanistan. If China is able to influence Pakistan in persuading the Taliban to pursue reconciliation with the internationally recognized Afghan government, then the SCO can also contribute significantly for Afghan reconstruction in the coming years. Continuing instability in Afghanistan will seriously affect Chinese integration plans in the region as well as the situation in Xinjiang. So it is in China's interest to use its leverage over Pakistan to find a solution.

Apart from the SCO, India will be concentrating on Afghanistan, Kazakhstan, Turkmenistan, and Azerbaijan for trade and energy cooperation. From the Indian point of view, extension of SAFTA to Central Asia could be useful. Already Afghanistan is a member, and Iran and China have been given observer status in the organization. Tajikistan, Uzbekistan, and Kazakhstan could be encouraged to be associated in the grouping. But the SAARC has to produce some concrete results to become attractive to Central Asians.

In a separate development, India has also set up a joint study group to explore the possibility of signing an FTA with the EAEU, which consists of Armenia, Belarus, Kazakhstan, Kyrgyzstan, and Russia. According to official sources, India hopes to make strong gains in areas such as pharmaceuticals, textiles, agriculture, and the energy sector and attract investments in its infrastructure sector through formal linkages with the EAEU.[40]

Air connections between India and the region are a prime example of tremendous business opportunities available when the Indian market is linked to Europe through Eurasia. For greater regional integration, air transportation is going to play an extremely important role in the coming years. Because land and rail corridors are going to take time (due to heavy investments and other

36. P. Stobdan, "Central Asia & China Relations: Implications for India," in *Asian Security and China 2000–2010*, ed. K. Santhanam and Srikanth Kondapalli (New Delhi: Shipra Publications, 2004), 343–358.

37. "India, Pakistan Become Full SCO Members," *The Hindu*, July 11, 2015, http://goo.gl/hdq1Cr.

38. "SCO to Consider Iran's Membership Bid after Lifting of UN Sanctions," Sputnik, December 29, 2015, http://goo.gl /NwGjcn.

39. "China Proposes Six Platforms for SCO Cooperation," Xinhua.net, December 15, 2015, http://news.xinhuanet.com /english/2015-12/15/c_134919792.htm.

40. "India Moves to Gauge Gains of a Free Trade Pact with Eurasian Union," *Hindu Business Line*, July 8, 2015, http:// goo.gl/Lfi31n.

political and security problems), air services at reasonable rates with reliable services could work wonders for the Eurasian region. Because air traffic into and out of the region may not be enough to sustain daily reliable services at economical rates, it has to be linked with the main traffic routes. Already there are about 30 direct weekly flights from India to all the important destinations in Afghanistan and Central Asia. These flights are operated, as low-cost carriers mostly by the Central Asian airlines to and from Delhi and Amritsar to Europe via Central Asian cities, like Tashkent or Ashgabat. Once airlines from Afghanistan are able to establish their European connections, Afghan airlines may be following the same route. In this way, Delhi could become the center of air corridors for the entire region. This is very much possible, as a major modernization program of Indian airports is already under way.

For India, transcontinental trade is much more important than trade only with the Eurasian region. For this reason, any plan of linking India with Europe through Eurasia will be much more valuable than just having some regional or subregional initiative. In this context, the plans for the Trans-Asian highway are very valuable to India. All Eurasian countries along with India and Pakistan are included in the plans for this highway. Implemented under the auspices of the United Nations Economic and Social Commission for Asia and the Pacific (UNESCAP), this project is a network of 141,000 km of roads crossing 32 Asian nations with linkages to Europe. Similarly countries of the region are involved in another UNESCAP project called the Trans-Asian Railway. As this network provides connectivity to 28 nations, a few more have joined later. The Transport Corridor Europe, Caucasus and Asia (TRACECA) is another program in which all Central Asians are involved. The European Commission, along with the governments in the region, formulated this 14-nation program in 1993. It starts in Eastern Europe and crosses Turkey, through Central Asia, to China and Afghanistan. In the last few years, new roads and railways are being built along the corridor. The Chinese OBOR project has taken some of these linkages as its own initiative. But this is the emerging scenario in which India has to operate, respond, and take its own initiatives.

INFLUENCE OF INDIAN ENGAGEMENT IN AFGHANISTAN ON EURASIA

Understanding that a peaceful and stable Afghanistan is crucial for regional stability, India is also trying to play an active role in postwar stabilization and development in that country. New Delhi has thus far pledged assistance worth $2 billion. Indian projects cover areas like road construction (the 218 km Zaranj-Delaram road), power (the transmission line from Pul-e-Khumri to Kabul), the Salma dam project, construction of the new Afghan parliament building, and many projects in the areas of agriculture, telecommunications, education, health, and capacity building. More than a thousand young Afghans also come to India every year on short- and long-term fellowships.[41]

---

41. For details of Indian projects in Afghanistan, see Gulshan Sachdeva, "The Reconstruction Issue in Afghanistan: Indian and Chinese Contribution," in *China and India in Central Asia: A New Great Game?*, ed. Marlène Laruelle et al. (New York: Palgrave Macmillan, 2010); and Gulshan Sachdeva, "The India-Afghanistan Development Partnership," in *India's Approach to Development Cooperation*, ed. Sachin Chaturvedi and Anthea Muleaka (New York: Routledge, 2016), 110–124.

To upgrade their relationship, Afghanistan signed its first-ever "strategic partnership" with India in 2011. Apart from increasing capacity building as well as sociocultural and educational linkages, the agreement pointed toward two major objectives. First, India agreed to assist in the training, equipping, and capacity-building programs for Afghan national security forces. Second, it recognized that regional economic cooperation is vital for the long-term economic prosperity of Afghanistan and the region as a whole. The agreement also created institutional mechanisms for implementation, consisting of an annual summit meeting, regular political consultations led by foreign ministries, and the establishment of a strategic dialogue on national security led by the two countries' national security advisers.[42] A few weeks after signing the agreement, a consortium of seven Indian companies led by the state-owned Steel Authority of India (SAIL) won a $10.3 billion deal to mine three iron ore blocks in the Bamiyan province, 130 km west of Kabul.[43]

In June 2012, the government of India in cooperation with the government of Afghanistan and the CII organized a successful investment summit on Afghanistan in Delhi. The main objective of the summit was to attract foreign investment, particularly in sectors like mining, hydrocarbons, infrastructure, telecommunications, agriculture, education, and health services.[44] This was perhaps the first time that a major summit on Afghanistan was being organized by a neighboring country mainly on its own initiative. In 2013, a similar conference was organized by the FICCI. In the Heart of Asia process, India leads the confidence-building measures focused on chambers of commerce as well as commercial opportunities.

With its strategic location, Afghanistan will always be important for India, particularly in the context of difficult India-Pakistan relations. However, Afghanistan's importance for India is much greater than normally perceived in this narrow context. Once Afghanistan becomes stable, trade through Pakistan and Afghanistan could also boost India's continental trade. With additional improvement in India-Pakistan relations, a significant portion of Indian trade (particularly from the landlocked northern states including Jammu and Kashmir) will be able to move through Pakistan and Afghanistan, which in turn would make many of the infrastructure projects planned for the region economically viable. These linkages will also transform small and medium industries and agriculture in Central Asia and Afghanistan.

First, though, a massive effort is needed to rebuild Afghanistan's transport network and economy. A few recent papers have outlined some concrete immediate and long-term measures that can soften the economic impact of military drawdown and create conditions for self-sustained growth.[45]

42. Indian MEA, "Text of Agreement on Strategic Partnership between the Republic of India and the Islamic Republic of Afghanistan," October 4, 2011, http://mea.gov.in/bilateral-documents.htm?dtl/5383/Text+of+Agreement+on+Strategic +Partnership+between+the+Republic+of+India+and+the+Islamic+Republic+of+Afghanistan.

43. Ruchira Singh and Utpal Bhaskar, "SAIL-Led Consortium Wins 3 Afghan Iron Ore Blocks," *Live Mint*, November 28, 2011, http://goo.gl/pB67lQ.

44. Gulshan Sachdeva, "The Delhi Investment Summit on Afghanistan," *IDSA Comment*, June 26, 2012, http://goo.gl /n8r0UQ.

45. S. Frederick Starr, with Adib Farhadi, *Finish the Job: Jump-Start Afghanistan's Economy: A Handbook of Projects*, Silk Road Paper (Washington, DC: Central Asia–Caucasus Institute & Silk Road Program, November 2012), http://www .silkroadstudies.org/resources/pdf/SilkRoadPapers/2012_11_SRP_StarrFarhadi_Afghanistan-Economy.pdf.

A major impediment in realizing this potential is the difficult relations between India and Pakistan. If trade stops in Pakistan, many road and other infrastructural projects will never become viable because of low volume. Direct linkages between Eurasia and India will also give a huge boost to all economies in the region, particularly to Afghanistan.

Earlier, it was thought that Afghanistan has very limited resources. The Afghanistan government in 2010 claimed, however, that the country has huge untapped mineral resources worth at least $3 trillion.[46]

Afghan and American officials have repeatedly talked about the New Silk Road (NSR). Since 2005, the idea has been discussed at many academic and policy forums, and was proclaimed official U.S. policy by the then secretary of state Hillary Clinton during a visit to India in October 2011. This strategy envisions an international trade, transit, and energy network linking the Central and South Asian economies through Afghanistan.[47] It was a good blueprint for Afghanistan, but unfortunately was mixed with regional geopolitics and exit strategies from Afghanistan.

On June 22, 2011, President Obama announced his drawdown plan from Afghanistan.[48] One month later, Secretary of State Hillary Clinton outlined the NSR at Chennai.[49] Many observers in the region looked at it as an integral part of the U.S. exit strategy from Afghanistan. The perception of U.S. withdrawal made countries in the region disinclined to take the NSR vision seriously. A few months later, all regional countries met at Istanbul for the November 2011 Heart of Asia conference. China, Russia, and Iran did not even allow the words "New Silk Road" to be mentioned in the declaration, even though all other large or small initiatives dealing with regional cooperation were referenced in the final declaration.[50]

Despite these setbacks, some major developments took place under the NSR heading. The Afghan-Pakistan Transit Trade Agreement (APTTA) was reached after years of negotiations and with active U.S. encouragement. Under the agreement, Afghanistan and Pakistan agreed to facilitate the movement of goods between and through their respective territories. Pakistan allowed Afghan exports to India through Wagah and to China through Sost/Tashkurgan. Similarly, Afghanistan allowed Pakistani trucks to reach Tajikistan, Turkmenistan, Uzbekistan, and Iran through its territories. At the moment, this is only a partial agreement as Afghan cargo is offloaded onto Indian trucks back to back at Wagah and trucks on return are not allowed to carry Indian exports back to Afghanistan. Despite its limited nature and serious initial problems in implementation, the agreement

---

46. "U.S., Afghan Study Finds Mineral Deposits Worth $3 Trillion," Bloomberg.com, January 29, 2011, http://goo.gl /oXdm8e.

47. S. Frederick Starr and Andrew C. Kuchins, *The Key to Success in Afghanistan: A Modern Silk Road Strategy*, Silk Road Paper (Washington, DC: Central Asia–Caucasus Institute and Silk Road Studies Program, May 2010), http://www .silkroadstudies.org/resources/pdf/SilkRoadPapers/2010_05_SRP_StarrKuchins_Success-Afghanistan.pdf.

48. Barack Obama, "Remarks by the President on the Way Forward in Afghanistan," White House, June 22, 2011, https://goo.gl/YAN1l1.

49. Hillary Rodham Clinton, "Remarks on India and the United States: A Vision for the 21st Century," U.S. Department of State, July 20, 2011, http://goo.gl/NQprsZ.

50. "Declaration of the Istanbul Process on Regional Security and Cooperation for a Secure and Stable Afghanistan," Heart of Asia—Istanbul Process, November 2, 2011, http://goo.gl/1lVJEg.

was seen as a major development in regional economic cooperation.[51] It also generated interest beyond Afghanistan and Pakistan. Initial work is under way on extending the agreement formally to Tajikistan.[52]

To make this initial small project into a serious regional economic force, it also needs to include Turkmenistan and Uzbekistan (and perhaps Iran). However, the project will be of very limited interest to the Central Asian countries if traffic to India is not allowed in both directions. Once Central Asians and India are included in an expanded APTTA, the region will be ready to take advantage of the emerging EAEU space within a few years. At the recent Heart of Asia Istanbul Process meeting in December 2015 in Islamabad, Indian foreign minister Sushma Swaraj indicated that India was willing to join the APTTA, and argued:

> The "Heart" of Asia cannot function if arteries are clogged. Nothing can benefit Afghanistan more immediately than full and direct overland access to India's markets to enable it to take advantage of the zero duty regime available to its exports to India. Similarly, if Afghan trucks could carry Indian products to markets in Afghanistan and Central Asia, that would be the best way to make trucking from Afghanistan cost-effective and viable, and bestow benefits to the whole region.[53]

51. Gulshan Sachdeva, "Afghanistan and Pakistan Sign Trade and Transit Agreement," *Central Asia–Caucasus Analyst* 12, no. 6 (September 2010), http://old.cacianalyst.org/?q=node/5392.

52. "Afghanistan, Pakistan, Tajikistan Near to Finalize Trilateral," *Bakhtar News*, April 13, 2015, http://goo.gl/uFl2P0.

53. Indian MEA, "Statement by External Affairs Minister at the Fifth Ministerial Conference of the Heart of Asia Istanbul Process," December 9, 2015, http://goo.gl/jz2kwU.

04

Conclusion

Economic growth in the last 25 years has broken all recent records in India. The strategic consequences of this economic performance are evident. Growth and outward orientation have helped India to reorient its traditional partnerships and forge new relationships, particularly in Asia. New Delhi in this period has signed more than two dozen strategic partnerships. Similarly, more than thirty trade and investment agreements are either signed or under negotiation. In 2014, Narendra Modi received a massive mandate mainly on the promise of good governance and development. Therefore, it is hoped that the reforms initiated by the previous governments may be not only carried out but also accelerated. During this period, India's economic links with most parts of Asia have been significantly strengthened.

The geopolitical importance of the Eurasian region has always been clearly understood by policymakers and analysts in India. New Delhi has long considered the region as part of its extended strategic neighborhood. After the collapse of the Soviet Union, when the New Great Game for energy resources and pipeline routes began in the region, India was a marginal player. Unlike other regional and outside powers, India was more concerned about political stability, as an unstable Eurasia could have created many security and strategic challenges. Because India had a limited presence in the region, it was attracted toward cooperative strategies with Russia, which it thought would remain the dominant player in the region because of historical and geographic factors.

Building on past linkages and goodwill, India has more recently developed strong political and developmental relations in the region, including "strategic partnerships" with Kazakhstan, Tajikistan, and Uzbekistan. Although India has been trying in the energy sector for quite some time, only recently have some concrete results started to emerge. India is slowly trying to enter the region in the areas of oil and gas and nuclear trade—key areas for the economies of the Central Asian states. If ArcelorMittal is considered "Indian," India has been a dominant player in iron and steel in the region for many years. In the textile sector, however, the Indian experience in Uzbekistan has not been very encouraging.

The increasing Chinese profile in Eurasia, both through the SCO and now through the OBOR, along with uncertainties surrounding Afghanistan have pushed India to formulate some new strategies in the region. This includes a new "Connect Central Asia" policy and high-profile visits to the region, including Prime Minister Modi's recent visit to all five Central Asian states.

The confusion and uncertainty created by the U.S. drawdown from Afghanistan have also pushed India to seek membership in the SCO. There is a possibility that the Chinese leadership may use the SCO to stabilize Afghanistan in the near future. In these circumstances, it would be wise for India to be part of the organization. India, anyway, was always positive about the potential for economic, energy, and transport projects growing out of the SCO.

India's current trade with the South Caucasus and Central Asia is very small, and likely to remain modest in the coming years. However, the importance of Eurasia for Indian trade should not be seen only in the context of very little regional trade with the smaller post-Soviet states. India's trade with the wider region, including Europe, the CIS countries, and Iran, Afghanistan, and Pakistan, is very significant. So even if 10 to 20 percent of this trade were conducted by road, a large volume of Indian trade would be passing through the Central Asia region. As a result, many planned infrastructure projects in the region would become economically viable, in turn creating further incentives for regional and subregional cooperation.

Despite the global slowdown of the past several years, the economies of states in the Eurasian region and South Asia are still doing relatively well. Growth in turn will be pushing policymakers to work for integration strategies. As a big, fast-growing economy, India is an attractive market for the smaller states of Eurasia. Regional economic integration is also important for sustainability for Afghanistan, as ultimately this country has to again play its traditional role of facilitating trade and commerce across its territory. So India is very positive about RECCA, the Istanbul Process, and the New Silk Road vision outlined by the Obama administration in the United States. Washington's strategic goals of stability in Afghanistan and promoting linkages between Central and South Asia have also coincided with India's expanding engagement in Afghanistan, and India's desire for a more prominent presence in Eurasia.

On the OBOR, India is still cautious. But it seems New Delhi will join some of its projects, and may also announce some counternarratives in the coming years.

In the absence of any other viable organization or initiative, the SCO may finally be becoming the forum for promoting interaction between the states of South and Central Asia in the near future. Another alternative would be the emergence of an entirely new organization from the existing structure of the RECCA, with a focus on Afghanistan. As the RECCA process itself has lost initiative to the Istanbul Process in recent years, the SCO has taken advantage of the resulting uncertainties.

Overall, compared with modest trade in South Asia, Central Asia, and the Caucasus, transcontinental trade through Eurasia is going to be much more important for India. As a result, plans for linking India with Europe through Eurasia will be much more valuable, rather than just thinking in some regional or subregional context. The UNESCAP plans for trans-Asian highways perfectly fit within this Indian framework. Different infrastructure plans, like the SAARC multimodel transport linkages, Central Asia Regional Economic Cooperation (CAREC) action plans, and the INSTC are all in a way different pieces of this grand design. India may also take advantage of some OBOR projects. Some of the capacities created by the Afghanistan-focused Northern Distribution Network (NDN) may also be utilized. In the long run, the Gwadar and Chabahar ports may also become complementary rather than competitive. Ultimately Indian trade volumes will be reaching Europe through a mix of these different schemes. As Iran is an important part of Indian strategy, India will continue to reenergize the INSTC. Further synergies through the SAARC and CAREC will improve its effectiveness and scope.

Despite serious problems in implementing regional integration strategies, such as continued tensions between India and Pakistan and the unsettled Afghanistan situation, there are some positive signs. These include APTTA, groundbreaking on TAPI, concrete plans for Chabahar, India's slow entry into Central Asian oil and uranium sectors, and the like. Any further improvement in ties between India and Pakistan or between the United States and Iran will improve India's maneuverability in the entire Eurasian region still further.

About the Author

Gulshan Sachdeva is a professor of European studies and director of the Europe Area Studies Programme in the School of International Studies at Jawaharlal Nehru University (JNU), New Delhi. He served as chairperson of the Centre for European Studies and director of the Energy Studies Programme at JNU. His research interests include the European Union, Eurasian integration, Afghanistan, development cooperation, and energy security. He headed the Asian Development Bank and the Asia Foundation projects on regional cooperation at the Afghanistan Ministry of Foreign Affairs in Kabul (2006–2010). He was Indian Council for Cultural Relations (ICCR) Chair on Contemporary India at the University of Leuven and visiting professor at the University of Warsaw, University of Trento, University of Antwerp, Corvinus University of Budapest, and Mykolas Romeris University (Vilnius). He has written many project reports for industry and government ministries and has published more than 100 research papers in academic journals and edited books. He holds an MA in economics from Punjabi University, an MPhil in Soviet studies from JNU, and a PhD in economic science from the Hungarian Academy of Sciences.

* 9 7 8 1 4 4 2 2 5 9 3 8 6 *